Charles Francis Browne, Frederick William Morton

Brush and pencil

Charles Francis Browne, Frederick William Morton

Brush and pencil

ISBN/EAN: 9783741174537

Manufactured in Europe, USA, Canada, Australia, Japa

Cover: Foto ©Andreas Hilbeck / pixelio.de

Manufactured and distributed by brebook publishing software (www.brebook.com)

Charles Francis Browne, Frederick William Morton

Brush and pencil

BRUSH AND PENCIL

*AN ILLUSTRATED MAGAZINE OF THE
ARTS OF TO-DAY*

EDITED BY
FREDERICK W. MORTON

VOLUME VIII
APRIL 1901 TO SEPTEMBER 1901

CHICAGO:
THE BRUSH AND PENCIL PUBLISHING COMPANY
1901

INDEX TO VOLUME VIII

		PAGE
AMERICAN ART INDUSTRIES V. REPRODUCTION OF PICTURES BY THREE-COLOR PROCESS . . . . . *Frederick W. Morton*		16
Eight Illustrations		
AMERICAN PATRON OF AMERICAN ART, AN	*Kirk D. Henry*	207
Seventeen Illustrations		
AMERICAN PICTORIAL PHOTOGRAPHY AT GLASGOW	*Allan C. MacKenzie*	169
Six Illustrations		
ART AND CRAFT OF THE MACHINE	*Frank Lloyd Wright*	77
ART EDUCATION IN AMERICA .	*W. M. R. French*	197
Twenty-three Illustrations		
ARTISTS' QUEST OF TYPES .	*Ellis T. Clarke* .	51
Twelve Illustrations		
ARTISTIC PHOTOGRAPHY OF HENRY TROTH	*Louis Albert Lamb*	281
Ten Illustrations		
BRIDGES, ARTISTIC AND INARTISTIC	*Henry T. Woodbridge*	322
Twelve Illustrations		
CAMERON, EDGAR—PAINTER	*Charles M. Towne*	177
Twelve Illustrations		
CANADIAN ART .	*Katherine V. McHenry* .	283
One Illustration		
CLEVER WORK OF STUDENTS		100
Four Illustrations		
COLOR SCHEME AT THE PAN-AMERICAN .	*Katherine V. McHenry* .	151
Ten Illustrations		
CONVENTION IN ART .	*Edgar Cameron* .	310
Fifteen Illustrations		
CULT OF GRANDPAS IN ART	*George Brandes* .	247
One Illustration		
ETCHINGS OF MRS. MARY NIMMO MORAN	*Morris T. Everett*	3
Seventeen Illustrations		
EVOLUTION OF A PICTURE—A CHAPTER ON STUDIES	*Edgar Cameron* .	121
Twenty-one Illustrations		
FREER, FREDERICK W.—PAINTER	*Frederick W. Morton*	289
Fifteen Illustrations		
HASSAM, CHILDE- IMPRESSIONIST	*Frederick W. Morton*	141
Ten Illustrations		
MAYER, HY.—HUMOROUS CARICATURIST	*David C. Preyer* .	161
Eleven Illustrations		

		PAGE
More Examples of Student Work		156
Four Illustrations		
New Departure in Study of Architectural Design	*Emil Lorch*	253
Twelve Illustrations		
The New York Art World—I	*David C. Preyer*	26
Twenty-one Illustrations		
New York Art World—II	*David C. Preyer*	91
Ten Illustrations		
Notable Western Exhibitions	*C. H. Harris*	63
Paintings at the Pan-American	*Herbert S. Granville*	223
Eight Illustrations		
Passing of a Famous Artist—Edward Moran	*Hugh W. Coleman*	188
One Illustration		
Philadelphia Water-Color Exhibition	*W. P. Lockington*	65
Eight Illustrations		
Plates—Colored		16, 24, 289, 304
Plates—Etchings		1, 7, 121, 133, 285
Plates—Paintings		29, 37, 61, 67, 69, 81, 85, 153, 177, 189, 233
Plates—Photographic		49, 173
Poetry and Pathos of Oriental Rugs	*W. G. Marquis*	301
Five Illustrations		
Pope, Alexander Painter of Animals	*Howard J. Cave*	105
Eight Illustrations		
Recent Work by Daniel Chester French	*Nelson R. Abbott*	43
Seven Illustrations		
Recent Work of Illustrators I	*Joseph Pennell*	72
Eight Illustrations		
Recent Work of Illustrators II	*Louis F. Braunhold*	136
Eight Illustrations		
Recent Work of Illustrators III	*Charles Robinson*	192
Eight Illustrations		
Recent Work of Illustrators IV	*M. H. Squire and E. Mars*	248
Four Illustrations		
Revival of Interest in Etching	*Morris T. Everett*	233
Twenty-two Illustrations		
Sculpture at the Pan-American	*William H. Holmes*	263
Twenty-four Illustrations		
Unique Turkish Coffee Set, A	*Charlotte Whitcomb*	135
One Illustration		
Work of the Younger Architects	*Robert C. Spencer*	113
Six Illustrations		

Brush and Pencil

Vol. VIII   APRIL, 1901   No. 1

THE ETCHINGS OF MRS. MARY NIMMO MORAN

When announcement was made in the fall of 1887 of an exhibition of the work of the women etchers of America, to be held at the Museum of Fine Arts in Boston, the surprise even of people well versed in art voiced itself in terms bordering closely on ridicule. The 4th of November came, and the public found, instead of a meager collection of "scratches on copper," a magnificent display of three hundred and eighty-eight plates, many of them of the highest order as regards both conception and execution. It was the first distinctive exhibition of the kind ever given. The etchings were discovered to be the work not of amateurs but of experts. Many of them were striking in their originality, and betrayed a force and skill of execution that compared favorably with the best efforts of men who had won fame with the needle.

MRS. MARY NIMMO MORAN
From a Photograph

Miss Gabrielle D. Clements, Miss Mary Cummings Brown, Mrs. Edith Loring Peirce Getchell, Mrs. Eliza Greatorex, Mrs. Anna Lee Merritt, Miss Margaret M. Taylor, and sixteen other talented women contributed to the exhibition. Among these was Mrs. Mary Nimmo Moran, who took rank both in number and quality of plates as the acknowledged leader of this select coterie—a position she held to the time of her death among women etchers. She exhibited fifty-four plates, diverse in character and theme, and her art was the subject of the most enthusiastic comment.

Mrs. Moran was not the pioneer woman etcher in America. Miss Cole, a sister of Thomas Cole, the artist, had etched a number of plates as early as the year 1844, and Mrs. Greatorex had etched her famous plate, "The Old Bloomingdale Tavern," in 1869. Mrs.

BRIDGE OVER THE DELAWARE
By Mrs. Mary Nimmo Moran
First Plate Etched by Artist, 1879

Moran's first plate, "Bridge over the Delaware," was not etched until 1879. When once her work had been begun, however, her position as an etcher was assured.

Her etching had an originality about it that gave evidence of a genius for that class of art production. It had a virile strength that set it in a class by itself. Her plates, as has frequently been said, would never reveal her sex, since they disproved the popular idea that the productions of a woman naturally betray feminine characteristics.

Her work was direct, emphatic, and bold to a point even that would not be attempted by male workers in the same line of art. Her own innate force of character, her broad, skillful treatment of her subjects, and her wise avoidance of affectation and incongruities resulted in the production of plates that had about them no suggestion of a woman's hand.

As a result, the public for a long time was misled into believing that M. Nimmo, the name Mrs. Moran signed to her plates, was the name of a man. Indeed, when the members of the New York Etching Club were invited to send examples of their work to the newly formed Society

SASSAFRAS GROVE, EASTHAMPTON
By Mrs. Mary Nimmo Moran

of Painter-Etchers of London, England, of which that prince of English etchers, Seymour Haden, was the leading spirit, she, with a number of others of the New York club, was elected a member, receiving a diploma signed by Queen Victoria herself. As her etchings were simply signed M. Nimmo—her maiden name—she was supposed to be a man, and for years she received communications from the London society addressed to her as such.

Mrs. Moran's interest in art dated from the time of her marriage, and her special interest in the etching-needle was due to an incident. A few words of biography, therefore, will be acceptable to the reader.

She was born in Strathaven, Scotland, in 1842, but coming to America in early life, she was soon completely identified with the country of her adoption. She became an enthusiastic admirer of America and a loyal American in every sense of the term. She finally settled in Philadelphia, where, in 1863, she was married to Thomas Moran. She immediately became his pupil, and worked under his direction with the greatest assiduity both in water-colors and in oil.

A WILLOWY BROOK
By Mrs. Mary Nimmo Moran

These early efforts she exhibited on various occasions at the

National Academy of Design, where they received a high tribute of praise. To-day her paintings are practically forgotten, since, when a start was once made with the needle, her fame as an etcher rapidly overshadowed the celebrity she attained in the first mediums in which she worked.

In 1867 Mr. and Mrs. Moran visited Europe, where they spent a period in studying the masterpieces of the most renowned artists collected in the various galleries, and where they made innumerable sketches of romantic scenery and of quaint and picturesque nooks and

CONWAY CASTLE, WALES
By Mrs. Mary Nimmo Moran

corners of the countries in which they sojourned. Mr. Moran was professedly an idealist. He had little interest in the commonplace, and less in the painful or depressing. He ignored the whims of fashion and the dictates of schools. The bent of his mind dictated a selection of subjects worthy by their beauty and their essential quality to be made themes for pictorial art, and his wife naturally caught her inspiration from him. Many of these European sketches were ultimately elaborated into their later works.

Mr. and Mrs. Moran removed to New York in 1871, and three years later they toured the western states. This trip was a tax on Mrs. Moran's energies, and when, in 1879, Mr. Moran decided to make another extended tour of the West for the purpose of painting

THE GOOSE-POND, EASTHAMPTON, L. I.
By Mrs. Mary Nimmo Moran
Diploma Etching in Royal Society of Painters-Etchers

GALLERY OF ETCHINGS
Plate Fourteen

THE ETCHINGS OF MRS. MARY NIMMO MORAN

THE MONTAUK HILLS, L. I.
By Mrs. Mary Nimmo Moran

some of its incomparable scenery, his wife wisely decided to remain at home.

This was the beginning of her interest in etching, which was taken up as a means of beguiling the time during her husband's absence. Before leaving New York the artist coated a number of copper-plates for his wife to experiment on. She had little knowledge of the art, only such as she had picked up by seeing her husband at work, and she thus began her career as an etcher without advice and without previous experience. It was primarily the enterprise of recreation, and neither Mrs. Moran nor her husband had any hope of ultimate success.

The value of Mrs. Moran's etchings is doubtless largely due to the independent way in which the fledgling devotee of the needle went to work. Denied guidance and assistance during her period of experimenting, and too ambitious and of too strong a character to be a mere copyist, she set out on the broad, free lines that subsequently made her famous. As a painter she had become a good draughtsman, and at the very outset of her career as an etcher she went direct to nature. It may be said here by way of parenthesis that of the long list of original etchings produced by Mrs. Moran, every one, without exception, was drawn on the plate direct from the subject.

When Mr. Moran returned from the West, the result of his wife's

OLD BRIDGE
By Mrs. Mary Nimmo Moran

initial efforts with the needle were a surprise to him. They were so original, so pronounced in their characteristics, so unlike anything he himself had done or had seen, that he scarcely knew whether to praise or condemn. Four of these first plates, however, were submitted to the New York Etching Club, and were promptly accepted for exhibition. They were warmly praised by the critics, and the unknown artist was elected a member of the club.

The difficulties overcome by Mrs. Moran during her period of unguided experimenting will scarcely be appreciated except by those who have undertaken a similar enterprise in art. In severing herself

A FLOWER-BOAT ON ST. JOHN'S RIVER, FLORIDA
By Mrs. Mary Nimmo Moran

from the ranks of copyists she cut herself off from much that would have been of vast assistance to her, and she thus forced herself to a hazardous development on strictly individual lines. Every artist knows that it is one thing to copy a picture and quite another to reproduce with fidelity a bit of landscape or a figure from the life. The copyist has all the lines laid down for him; the original artist has been the interpreter of nature. The copyist, therefore, has only to follow, with as much precision as may be, the outlines and shadings of his master. Painting or etching direct from nature, on the other hand, throws the artist upon his own resources.

It is an old story of the class-room, that while practice direct from nature is productive of self-reliance, and is essential to every student who wishes to do work of value, nature is not always a safe guide to the uninitiated. Accuracy of draughtsmanship, quickness of eye, and a correct estimate of sky values, tones, and half-tones are necessary prerequisites of the painter or etcher who does work direct from nature, and the novice who essays efforts in this way courts a danger he would escape if he were under the guidance of a teacher.

It is also to be borne in mind that a wrong stroke with the pencil can be erased easily, or a wrong stroke with the paint-brush can be corrected or covered up with little trouble. When once, however, a line has been etched by the needle, its effacement is a more difficult matter. The freer the expression of the etcher, the more beautiful, as a rule, is his plate; and the more evidence there is of studied changes, the less happy is the result. That Mrs. Moran should have begun as she did, a mere unskilled novice, and should have succeeded

POINT ISABEL, FORT GEORGE ISLAND, FLORIDA
By Mrs. Mary Nimmo Moran

in producing such admirable effects is an enviable tribute to her genius.

As Mrs. Schuyler Van Rensselaer long since pointed out, Mrs. Moran found her true artistic voice only when she took up the etching-needle. She discovered in it a means of expression suited to her intense personality. She recognized the aptitude she had for this peculiar form of work. From the outset she became a systematic, industrious, and unassuming student, and by choice she became an exponent of rural scenes.

She had a quick sense of the beautiful and the picturesque, and no dearth of artistic conceptions. Her favorite method of work was to take her copper-plate and etch her chosen subject, practically to the last stroke, in some secluded corner or under a sheltering tree, having the inspiration of the scenes she was depicting ever before her; and the plates herewith reproduced are sufficient witness that her method was well chosen.

AN OLD HOMESTEAD, EASTHAMPTON, L. I.
By Mrs. Mary Nimmo Moran

Speaking of Mrs. Moran, S. R. Koehler, than whom American etchers never had a warmer friend or a more enthusiastic advocate, said some years ago: "In etching, Mrs. Moran finds a language that accords entirely with her ideas and modes of expression. She treats her subjects with poetical disdain of detail, but with a firm grasp of the leading truths that give force and character to her work. While her etchings do not display the smoothness that comes from great mechanical dexterity, her touch is essentially that of the true etcher—nervous, vigorous, and rapid, and bitten in with a thorough appreciation of the relations of the needle and acid, preferring robustness of line to extreme delicacy. The influence of her husband's example is plainly visible in all she does, even in the restlessness that pervades most of her plates. But with this peculiarity are also coupled the other admirable qualities of Mr. Moran's work—the vivid suggestion of color, and the feeling of life and air, as of a sunshiny but windy day when cloud-shadows are scattered all over the landscape and break up its unity."

In Mr. Koehler's opinion "Twilight," a plate of extraordinary power and beauty, in which the effect has been heightened by the use of the roulette and by stoning, but without any sacrifice of either strength or harmony, is an etching of sufficient value to establish the artist's claim to rank among the masters of landscape etching.

The reader can glean from the accompanying reproduction of this plate some idea of its correct values and of its rich effects. It is simply a scene at Easthampton, long the home of Mrs. Moran, and to few, perhaps, would have the poetic significance it had to the artist. The plate has the delicate softness incident to the way in which it was made. Night is just settling upon the glow of day, and the peculiar atmosphere of the hour is depicted with a fidelity to nature rarely equaled.

"Easthampton Barrens" is another of the artist's plates of quiet Easthampton scenery into which she has infused a poetic charm. This plate and "Bridge over the Delaware," already referred to, have an added interest as being two of the four original etchings made in 1879 that were sent to the New York Etching Club, and that first gained her recognition as a master of the needle. Indeed, many have considered her experimental plates as among the finest she produced.

"Solitude," a placid pool of water surrounded by a clump of trees, whose bare trunks are sharply outlined against the sky, is one of her best, as it is one of her strongest, etchings. "The Goose Pond" is regarded as less original in motive, but it is a remarkable piece of work, and is notable from the fact that it was the diploma etching that secured her election to the Society of Painter-Etchers of London. In this plate the treatment of the water and the atmosphere are especially noteworthy.

The collection of etchings accompanying this article is the most

TWILIGHT, EASTHAMPTON, L. I.
By Mrs. Mary Nimmo Moran

comprehensive ever published of Mrs. Moran's work. It gives a fair idea of her versatility, of her favorite themes, and of her peculiar method of treatment. "The Haunted House" is a plate of wonderful power, showing what a wealth of poetic charm a skillful artist of sentiment and feeling can infuse into a picture of what the average spectator would consider devoid of beauty and interest. "Between the Gloaming and the Murk" has been called an idyllic pastoral, beautifully expressed in the soft tints of monochrome. It is simply another picture of a landscape dying in the night. One can but feel that the scene in fact is barren even to the repellent, while through

EASTHAMPTON BARRENS
By Mrs. Mary Nimmo Moran

the witchery of line and the softness of mezzotint the picture is fascinating.

And so with the rest of Mrs. Moran's plates. They are for the most part unpretentious scenes whose beauty she discovered and recorded. Many of them are nooks in the vicinity of her Easthampton home, as, for instance, "A Willowy Brook," "An Old Bridge," "The Montauk Hills," "Sassafras Grove," and "Summer." They depict a hillside, a pool, a clump of trees, a tumble-down ramshackle, a stretch of marsh-land, or something equally simple, and equally devoid of interest save when seen by an artist who had poetry enough in her soul to make such scenes replete with meaning and beauty.

In some of her work she broke away from her favorite subjects and boldly took up new themes, but her mastery of her art invested these plates with quite as much interest as it did those of scenes with which she was more familiar. This is the case with etchings like "Conway Castle, Wales," and the Florida scenes she etched in 1887, as for instance, "A Flower Boat on the St. John's River" and "Point Isabel, Fort George Island," in which she succeeded in catching the true spirit of the southern clime. This last etching is simply a desolate stretch of wave-washed strand, with scarce a shrub or tree to

SUMMER, EASTHAMPTON, L. I.
By Mrs. Mary Nimmo Moran

break the monotony. One almost wonders that the artist had the hardihood to select a scene so barren and invest it with the elements of the winsome. The plate, however, is extremely successful, and is regarded by many as among her best.

For twenty years, from her first hazardous beginnings to her death in September, 1899, Mrs. Moran was loyal to her first ideals and true to her own strong individuality. Never for a moment did she allow fads or fashion to warp her judgment, or cause her to wander from the path on which she started when she undertook unaided to develop her art. At the outset of her career she was honored by having her experimental plates admitted to the exhibition of the New York Etching Club, and in winning her way to membership in the London Society of Painter-Etchers, and as late as 1893 she was accorded a medal and a diploma for etchings at the Columbian Exposition in Chicago. From first to last her work showed no evolution or marked change. She never regarded herself as a professional, but looked upon her art as a pleasant accomplishment, and the excellence she attained was simply the outcome of her love of the art. MORRIS T. EVERETT.

HAUNT OF THE MUSKRAT
By Mrs. Mary Nimmo Moran

AMERICAN ART INDUSTRIES—V

REPRODUCTION OF PICTURES BY THREE-COLOR PROCESS

One of the most remarkable achievements of recent years in the art of printing is the perfection of the three-color process, by which paintings or other colored pictures can be reproduced, often with absolute and always with approximate fidelity to the originals. To-day this class of art work is so common as to have lost its novelty. Colored reproductions of pictures are used in books, in magazines, in business circulars, as supplements to newspapers. One finds them everywhere, and often with a degree of excellence that makes them marvels of beauty.

To the public, however, the manner of their production is one of the mysteries of the art industries. To the uninitiated the three-color process is little more than a name for an admirable result. In a general way it is known that pictures such as the two accompanying this article require three printings, and that the different inks used are red, blue, and yellow. But beyond this the knowledge of the average layman does not extend.

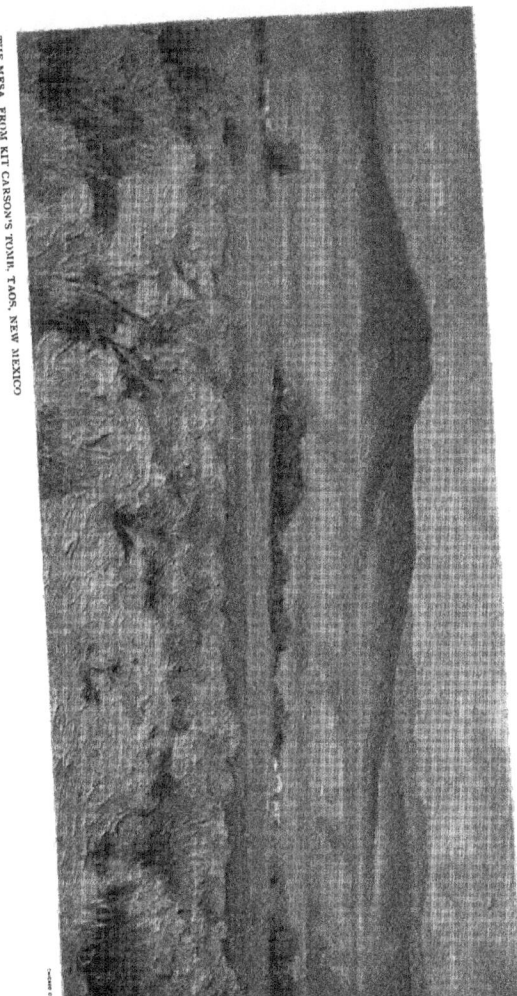

THE MESA, FROM KIT CARSON'S TOMB, TAOS, NEW MEXICO
BY J. H. SHARP

If he should see the three plates from which the different printings are made, they would look so nearly alike that he could not distinguish one from the other, and yet the combined impressions of the three plates, each imparting to the page its one color, give every variation of hue used by the artist, who in painting the picture laboriously mixed his paints on a palette to produce the desired effect. By what trick of mechanism can three metal plates be so manipulated as to preserve faithfully the outlines of a picture and maintain intact all of its color values—the reds, for instance, merging by proper gradations into russets or pinks, the purples fading into violets or blues, the oranges changing into yellows or buffs, and the greens varying from the intensest to the weakest shades?

The accompanying color-prints—no apology is needed for their reappearance in BRUSH AND PENCIL, since they are designed here to subserve a specific purpose—are admirable illustrations of the artistic results obtained by this process. Neither of the pictures gives more than a mere hint of the three colors used in its production. The red, blue, and yellow inks are disguised, blended into an artistic aggregation of other shades. It is the purpose of this article to explain how mechanism pure and simple duplicates the studied, painstaking efforts of the artists.

Colored photography has been the dream of a century, ever since Ritter, of Jena, noticed that the various rays of the spectrum differed considerably in their action upon chloride of silver. This observation was made in 1801, and young as three-color printing is, it is the direct but tardy fruit of this casual observation. To trace the work of different experimenters here would be out of place, and a minute technical discussion of theories and practices would be equally foreign to the purpose of the article. Only enough detail, therefore, will be given to explain the underlying principle and make clear the various steps in the production of a picture by the three-color process.

The old division of white light into its primary constituent colors was violet, indigo, blue, green, yellow, orange, and red, but it is a truism of to-day that of these seven four may be discarded. The remaining three, blue, yellow, and red, make white light, and by the proper mixture of these three every conceivable color can be produced. This fact is the basis of the three-color process in printing, and the men who perfected the method had before them the task of devising a mechanical way of mixing inks of the three colors named on a page so that the overlapping of the colors would produce the proper shades in the proper places, thus preserving the details of the picture as a drawing and at the same time correctly reproducing its color scheme.

A close inspection of the accompanying color-plates—"The Mesa, from Kit Carson's Tomb, Taos, New Mexico," by J. H. Sharp, and "The Bal Bullier, Luxembourg Gardens," by Frank X. Lyendecker—

in which the most delicate shades are reproduced with remarkable faithfulness to the originals, might naturally give one an exaggerated idea of the difficulty attending the feat of stamping red, blue, and yellow on a sheet of paper so as to produce the results obtained. Really the feat is not such a difficult one.

It is a fact well known to the student of physics that red light and green light unite to make yellow, that blue light and green light produce peacock blue, that blue light and yellow light make white, and so on with different results throughout the various combinations to which the three primary colors and their modifications are susceptible, the tint or resulting color depending upon the relative proportions of the constituent colors that enter into its composition. It is also a well-known fact that white light can be sifted so as to strain out, if one may use the phrase, certain of the constituent elements so as to give the transmitted portion of the light an entirely different hue. Here, then, was the basis for experimenting.

HALF-TONE FROM COLORED ORIGINAL
Made with White Light

If by some clever means it were possible to take a photograph of a colored object and sift out the blue and yellow elements of the white light by which it is ordinarily seen, the result would be a picture in which the red constituent of the light played an exaggerated part. If a similar photograph were taken and the red and yellow elements were sifted out, the blue element would be exaggerated in the picture. If, again, another photograph were taken and the red and blue elements were sifted out, the yellow element would predominate in the result. It will thus readily be seen that, in a sense, it would require a superposition of the three pictures thus taken one upon the other to restore the proper values of the different colors in the original.

In other words, we would have three transcripts of a colored object, each lacking something to be found in the other two. If these three transcripts, therefore, were transformed into three printing surfaces, we might reasonably expect them to stamp the three primary colors on a page in the proper proportions so that the superposition of the three colors one upon the other would produce the varying shades of the original object. That is exactly what is done in three-color printing.

The accompanying color-plates were printed from three half-tone plates, made, as just said, in such a way that each emphasizes one of the primary colors and subordinates the other two. The art of making a half-tone plate, such as the illustrations in BRUSH AND PENCIL are printed from, was fully explained in a recent issue of the magazine, and need not here be repeated in detail. It is only necessary to recall that the half-tone is simply a metal plate whose surface consists of innumerable dots and intervening spaces, the dots being larger and the intervening spaces narrower in the dark portions of the picture, and the dots being smaller and the intervening spaces wider in the light portions.

YELLOW PLATE FOR COLOR WORK
Made with Violet Light

The half-tone plates used in three-color work are essentially of the same character, and so far as the mere mechanical process is concerned are made practically in the same way. The main difference is in the lights used in making the three plates.

In the actual production of a three-color print, the yellow is printed first, then the red, and lastly the blue. In making the photograph

HALF-TONE PLATE FROM COLORED ORIGINAL.
Made with White Light

YELLOW PLATE FOR COLOR WORK
Made with Violet Light

RED PLATE FOR COLOR WORK
Made with Green Light

BLUE PLATE FOR COLOR WORK
Made with Red Light

of the colored object from which the yellow plate is made, violet light is used, since this color cuts off or reduces the other colors found in the original. In making the photograph for the red plate, green light is used, since this cuts off the other colors and emphasizes the red; and in making the photograph for the blue plate red light is used, since this reduces the other colors and emphasizes the blue. We have now three photographs with the color values distorted, which are called color record negatives.

In making these record negatives the violet, green, and red light is furnished simply by inserting between the object and the lens of the camera a perfectly even plate of glass of the requisite color, or a flat jar containing a liquid colored to the proper tint. The rays of white light reflected from the object photographed are sifted by the colored medium through which they pass and fall upon the sensitized surface of the plate prepared to receive the impression in such a way as to produce the disturbance of color values.

RED PLATE FOR COLOR WORK
Made with Green Light

From these record negatives, record positives are then made, just as positives are made from negatives in an ordinary case of photography, and from these record positives half-tones are made, just as has already been described in these pages. We now have three plates with good printing-surfaces, each tolerably faithful to the original colored picture in point of outline, but each essentially different from the other in its shadings.

The impression of one plate is printed directly upon the other, the utmost care being taken to preserve the register; that is, to make a given point in one impression fall exactly upon the same point in the others. The impression with yellow ink is made, and allowed to dry. On this is printed the red impression, the superposition of the red upon the yellow largely killing the first color and markedly modifying the red itself. Upon this combination of red and yellow the blue impression is made, and the picture is again transformed. The red overlapping the yellow destroys the first color, except where it should remain comparatively strong, and the blue overlapping the two previous colors supplies the remaining constituent of the white light by which the spectator sees the picture.

The result is that yellow, blue, and red only appear in the finished picture where they appeared in the originals reproduced. In all other portions of the picture, by mere superposition of one upon another, the three primary colors have disappeared. In some portions they have been changed into entirely different colors, in others they have been modified into shades or tones of some one of the primary colors used.

BLUE PLATE FOR COLOR WORK
Made with Red Light

In "The Mesa," for instance, the reader will notice delicate and pronounced greens. No green ink was used in the printing, the greens resulting in the picture from the mixing of the three colors actually used. The mountain-peaks in the distance are clothed in purples of different shades. These tones again result from combinations.

In the "Bal Bullier," the stonework of the fountain appears in the picture a natural stone color, while the horses and the reflection of the horses in the water are a pronounced green. Both these colors, as well as the grayish blue water in the immediate foreground and the twinkling white lights in the background, are derived colors. One might suppose that the gas and the electric lights in the distance were simply the white paper showing through the various impressions. In reality, the white is simply the superposition of red and blue upon yellow.

For the purpose of comparison, two sets of four plates each of the same picture are supplied. In each set, one plate, so marked, is simply a half-tone showing the result when the various colors of the original are properly co-ordinated by white light in the manufacture of the plate. The other three in each set are, respectively, the yellow, red, and blue plates made for the actual work of producing a colored reproduction. It needs but a casual inspection by the reader to see the most pronounced differences in the shadings of the different plates.

In the picture of the peasant-girl, for instance, the mountain in the distance is barely visible in the red plate, while in the blue plate it is very pronounced. In the finished picture the mountains are a hazy blue. The stonework in the red plate is very light, while in the yellow plate it is comparatively dark. In the finished picture the stonework is a brownish gray. A very marked difference will be noticed in the shading of the foliage at the base of the tree, it being faint in the red plate, darker in the blue, and darkest in the yellow. In the finished picture red is almost eliminated; the foliage is russet where the yellow plate is densest and green where the deepest shadings of the blue plate have fallen.

And so in the comparative plates of the woman's head. The half-tone plate shows the various colors of the original properly co-ordinated. In the other three plates the emphasis given, respectively, to the yellow, blue, and red can easily be detected. Naturally, the face of the picture should be white. In the half-tone made with white light the face is white. In each of the other plates the face is dark, yet when the red and blue plates are superimposed upon the yellow plate in the process of printing the union of the three makes white. Consequently, while the face is dark in the impressions given by each of these plates separately, the result of all three impressions, one upon the other, produce a white face.

To burden this article with the details that would have to be taken into consideration by the practical worker in producing a colored reproduction would be but to confuse the reader. A popular account for the intelligent reader, and not an exhaustive explanation, is all that is intended. One point of detail, however, further than has been given must not be omitted.

In making the half-tones for the different color-plates, apart from filtering the light in making the color record negatives, the main point of departure from the ordinary method of half-tone manufacture is in the fact that the screens for the different plates are set at different angles. It will be remembered that in making a half-tone plate the surface of the picture is broken up into dots and spaces—the tooth to

"THE BAL BULLIER," LUXEMBERG GARDENS

make the impression upon the paper—by being photographed through a finely ruled pane of glass called a screen. In making the three plates for color-work it has been found that the best results are obtained when the screen for the second plate is turned to an angle of thirty degrees from the first, and the screen for the third plate to thirty degrees from the second.

There is thus less interference with the colors, the red, blue, and yellow dots of the different half-tones falling in such a way as to produce the most brilliant and luminous effect. The massing of colors by superposition is in no wise affected by thus setting the lines of the screens at an angle, since at whatever angle the screen may be set, the dense portions of the photograph will be dense in the plate, while, on the other hand, the different colored dots falling minutely out of register give life to the picture and enhance by its beauty.

In conclusion, it may be said, by way of recapitulation, that every colored picture, like the two accompanying this article, requires in all fifteen operations. First, it is necessary to take three color record negatives to emphasize each of the three primary colors in a single photograph. From these three record positives must be made as in ordinary photography. Then three screen negatives are made, followed by the manufacture of three half-tone plates. And lastly, there must be three printings, one each with the three different colored inks. There are processes by which some of these intermediate steps may be eliminated, as, for instance, the grain process. These short methods, however, are the exception, the full number of steps being usually taken in ordinary art and commercial three-color work.

FREDERICK W. MORTON.

JAPANESE HAND-CUT STENCIL
Collection of H. Deakin

THE NEW YORK ART WORLD

The time has long gone by when a portly London alderman at a Lady Sheriff's luncheon announced with indignation that at Carlton House he had seen "the rooms filled with picters," and my Lady Mayoress exclaimed: "How vulgar; it spoils the paper."

The groveling commercialists, the purse-proud sons of wealth, and the more humble admirers of the beautiful in color and line now equally enjoy the sublime pathos the chaste grace, the dignified sentiment, the poetic expression of art in all its phases, and love to be surrounded by it. And many have been the opportunities of late offered to the New York public to view exhibitions of excellent artistic properties—an admirable substitute for their possession.

Of note has been the large number of one-man shows. We have had George McCord, whose versatile mind seems to have a fuller grasp and wider power of expression. A score of his canvases seen together portrayed Dutch scenes, Maine coasts, English river views, French *paysagerie*, and all fully carrying the atmosphere of the locality, with mellow tones, delicate luminosity, or Turneresque glow. Another painter whose forward stride has called attention to his work recently exhibited, is the marine artist, F. K. M. Rehn. It is easy to obtain a resemblance of broken running-water by tricks and dexterities—to delineate successfully its weight and mass, as well as the thick, creamy, curdling, overlapping foam, places one not far below the mark of a Backhuyzen or a Courbet. This is the place Rehn now occupies.

There have been shown also a collection of works by Wyant and Inness, reminiscent indeed, of wide range of importance, yet leaving a grateful taste. If anywhere, the similarity of artistic development of

"A QUESTION"
By G. R. Barse, Jr.

Inness and Corot came here to the fore. Both passed through three periods, the last being so superb in its productions that we would willingly forget the earlier stages. Wyant seems to have been less marked in his changing. His was more a natural growth, that amplified itself without departing from its first bud-opening. In their own

PORTRAIT OF MRS. M. E. PORTER
By R. W. Vonnoh

method of looking at nature both revealed its visual aspect in differing ways with equal skill.

It was fortunate that at the same time an exhibition was running of the wood interiors of R. M. Shurtleff, a man whose works some day will be ranked of the highest. How fervently it might be wished that the multitude were sufficiently enlightened to recognize greatness in the flesh instead of in the shroud. How many men have spent their days in squalor whose names are entered now upon the roll of fame. It is not as bad as that with Shurtleff; and yet it must be said

A WOOD NYMPH
By Edward Potthast

that where some years hence the crowd will bid, and bid high, for his magnificent wood temples, virginal forest stretches, pure, breathing the ozone of vigorous life, there are now only the real art-lovers and connoisseurs who quietly collect his canvases, even as Wyant's and Martin's were put by years ago.

Our figure painters, not too many in number, have been added to by the accession of a young English-woman who has just settled among us. Miss Ethel Wright has acquired an enviable reputation in London art circles, where her work has repeatedly attracted attention in the Royal Academy exhibitions. She has a singularly virile touch and a delightful color sense, which, combined with dramatic presentation, result in most attractive and highly artistic compositions.

Turn now to portraiture. We have had shown the work of Irving R. Wiles, of Zorn, and a few others. Mr. Wiles is an uneven workman. Some of his figures look stilted, are hard in color, and lack the delicate suppleness of flesh-tints. Portraiture resembles

EARLY SNOW
By H. Bolton Jones

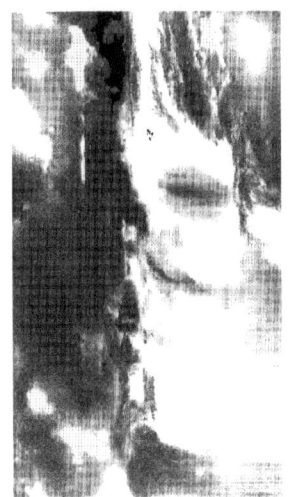

sculpture in calling for the most intense and concentrated force of the imaginative faculty. Any clever sketcher may catch a likeness to be recognizable. The height of portraiture is, however, in some mysterious way to give the substance of the person's character, "the form and pressure of his mind," so far as these inner features are stamped on the outward. Wiles does sometimes succeed in doing this, and the quality of the full-length, in an unfinished state, of a young lady leads one to suspect that he might succeed oftener if he did not elaborate so much, which causes his more carefully finished work to become finical. One

MAID OF THE HILLS
By J. G. Brown

A PEASANT VILLAGE
By Will Robinson

might say, the soul is brushed out. To my mind his portrait of W. Ritschel, a young man in a tennis-suit, at the Academy was one of the best of human counterfeits.

Zorn stands

alone among our foreign visitors bidding for commissions. His is an uncompromising art, without flattery, true, yet delicately ignoring disturbing imperfections. A full-length of a reclining woman, at whose side a Scotch collie is sitting, is a marvelous piece of work of

IN THE PARK
By Samuel Isham

great power. Still better is he in his men's portraits, where grace and strength are limned with skill and dignity.

Harry Franklin Waltman, recently returned from Paris, but originally hailing from beyond the Alleghenies, is another portrait painter whose brush depicts with certain touch the character of his sitters. His work reveals technical proficiency acquired by a thorough study of the old masters, while yet his presentation gives his portrait a modern envelope. Mrs. Margarete Austin, who before coming to the metropolis has painted many prominent people in Chicago, Milwaukee, and Washington, has exhibited some miniatures. She is a splendid colorist, and has the remarkable gift of infusing in the dainty "painting in little" a breadth and largeness of conception rarely found in this delicate work. Her backgrounds offer a fitting setting to the lifelike presentments.

The stirring of art interests as here recorded was preceded by a National Academy exhibition which was better than for many years. The new blood is working. There is pursued a more liberal policy toward outsiders, and somehow the Academicians do not presume too much, as in the past. True, all is not yet as it might be. The jury of admission with commendable fairness admitted the work of the younger men, but it must be said that the hanging committee to a measure negatived this fairness by relegating to the small chambers some important canvases, which for size, if for nothing else, required as

"TO THE MANNER BORN"
By J. H. Witt

THE MILL AT BRINTON'S BRIDGE
By Walter Clark

A VENETIAN HOME
By George H. Smillie

well as deserved a place in the larger galleries, to change places with many of the smaller and unimportant compositions of older men. There was, for instance, "Splitting Fish," by J. W. Hawthorne, a subject with bold grasp, vigorously handled. A group of men are engaged in the occupation indicated in the title; the characteristic attitude and fullness of life, as well as the *natura morte*, were powerful. Maybe the technique here and there might have been questioned in the fuller light. Nevertheless the work would have risen in the estimation of the visitor.

The same may be said of the large canvas "The Dying Sioux," by Van D. Perrine, which in its monotone forced itself away from its small surroundings. And again in the same little room there was hung, skied, "Sevillana," by F. Luis Mora. We do not have sufficient figure

AUTUMN SUNSET, PELHAM BAY
By Lockwood De Forest

men to slight these coming ones. In this Spanish fandango there was comprised grace of line, homogeneous composition, and striking yet well-modulated color. Still, many must have overlooked this, one of the best things of the whole show.

NEAR EGREMONT
By O. P. Black

What is the cause of this? Is it a manifestation of that professional jealousy toward younger men of which the older ones are often accused? There comes to mind an incident along the same line which I learned a few weeks ago. Two wealthy men from out of town, who had just finished building new homes, came to purchase a number of paintings, and having been advised, had decided to procure works by American artists. An amateur friend suggested that they should

REPOSE
By Matilda Browne

meet a well-known artist, and the quartet sat down to dinner to discuss what painters should be represented in the collections. But alas! every name mentioned was so thoroughly roasted by the professional that the buyers, in disgust, changed their minds, and next day bought only foreign works. This is a sad story, *mes amis peintres;*

UNMASKED
By Herbert A. Lavy

the thought will not down as expressed by old Gray in "The Poet and the Rose":

"I hate the man who builds his name
On ruins of another's fame."

The Academy was a good show, for all that. The prize-pictures were singled out with tolerable judgment, which, however, was not indorsed by all connoisseurs. The Academy was especially rich in portraiture, and marked vast progress in the landscape art.

But alackaday! Why is it that some heralds, with daring blasts on tin trumpets, will issue forth to the unheard-of persecution of the Academy, which means well, and is now doing better? The yearly

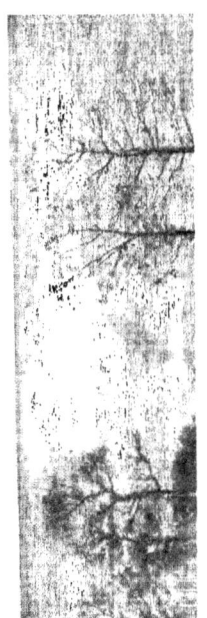

exhibition is the occasion of these malignant writers with bad taste to mark down the Academy for public sport, and many open-mouthed blockheads will join in the chase. The specious attacks of these pamphleteers declare them to be more anxious to be singularly fallacious than customarily instructive.

The portraits at this annual show were, with some exceptions, of notable value. There were Frederick P. Vinton's "Mr. John Harsen Rhoades," of faultless brushing and fine character; and the excellent canvas, "Portrait of Mrs. M. E. Porter," by R. W. Vonnoh. Here is a man who will rival Sargent.

Our woman painters come to the front. Cecilia Beaux has attained an enviable reputation; she was not represented, but another woman portraitist made here a distinct impression. She is Miss Clara T. McChesney, who in the portrait of Artist Newman has limned a superb canvas. It is a breathing image of a kindly old man with the light of pleasantry in his eye, of which the title, "A Good Story," tells the secret. The technical qualities of this portrait are

PORTRAIT OF JAMES M. HART
By Mary Theresa Hart

faultless; the black hat, set jauntily on the white locks, comes distinctly out of the dark background, the pose is natural, the whole painted with a free brush *con amore*. And the joke that goes around this portrait is, that a moral censor, whose modesty is a candle to his merit, refused to have it reproduced in a series of famous portraits because poor Newman has a beer-mug in his hand.

The Misses Hart contributed a portrait study of two figures, which received a prize, but which was somewhat too decorative in conception and not quite decorative enough by its lack of completeness. Miss Mary Theresa Hart's portrait of James M. Hart was much better. Miss Elizabeth F. K. van Elten, now studying in Paris, sent also an excellent portrait of her father, the Academician, Kruseman van Elten. Joseph H. Boston's decorative conception, which he called "Olive Tone," was a portrait in its human qualities, while Carroll Beckwith contributed two female faces, of which "In Royal Robes," the portrait of a young girl, was exquisite in handling and color scheme.

THE DEFIANCE
By De Cost Smith

Comparatively few figure-subjects were shown, but here there is, at the least, most progress discernible. It is the Nemesis of art that we must have the old-time senilities of the men who really bring all the odium on the Academy. Younger men came, however, to the fore. Besides the three already mentioned, there was E. Potthast, who showed a "Wood-nymph," which lacked the aerial filminess of this mythical phenomenon, and was altogether too solid. Nevertheless it was a most charming figure, of rare decorative quality. For forceful painting commend me to Ben Eggleston's "Summer and Autumn," two full-length draped female figures, life size, that in brush-work showed the swing and strength of a master hand, while the values of the white gowns were skillfully and truthfully given. Even this painting was, I will not say sent out into the cold, but like *vox clamantis in deserto*, the hanging committee banished it to a little room. It deserved a better fate.

All these are of the younger men. They have what must be called individual style. Commonplace and superficiality may withdraw attention from good work for a time; the crowd of incapables will surely be relegated to the rear, hanging committees to the contrary notwithstanding. The Thomas B. Clarke prize was worthily awarded to William Fair Kline for "The Flight into Egypt," presented in the conventional manner, it is true, but with such poetic charm, such dignity of characterization, such expressive feeling and impeccable brushing that it formed a striking feature. One small canvas should not be overlooked. It was by Elizabeth F. Bonsall, "Two's Company, Three's None," showing a girl and kittens, which was dainty and lovable, with sure management of the whites.

And then the landscapes. American landscape art is gradually evolving into an art expression, distinctly its own. Even the foreign influences which wrought upon our painters in the past have served to give art manifestation its right expression, from which individual conception has cropped forth with ever-increasing distinctness. Thus we saw at Paris last year the accomplishment of our fond hopes, and the American landscape painter was accorded the honor of being the purest portrayer of nature's glories. And this year's Academy gave ample credit to his prowess.

THE PORT, ST. MALO
By Carlton T. Chapman

E. Irving Couse places figures in his compositions which are part and parcel of their settings, yet he is by eminence a landscape painter. W. Elmer Schofield, in his "Winter Evening," associates the onlooker with the plain truth of the earth and the fullness thereof in its garment of sleep. There is naïvety and grace in the bits of scenery which Charles Warren Eaton portrays; while George H. Smillie arranges his snatches of hill and dale with artistic intent.

"The more the artist charms, the more the thinker knows," says Schiller somewhere. To stand before a canvas painted by Fred W. Kost, as we saw here in his "Frosty Morning," there is conveyed the feeling of outdoors and the knowledge of the sublimity of nature which ever proclaims that "God made the country and man the town." Such like impression carries one from the work of Leonard Ochtman; of John Noble Barlow; of A. T. van Laer, whose progress is certain;

PORTRAIT
By A. B. Sewell

of the doughty Edward Gay, who is renewing his youth; of Walter Clark, whose "Mill at Brinton's Bridge" is so full of sunlight; and of John G. Saxton, another young man of great promise. Robert D. Ganley, still another newcomer, unveils the mountain mystery of the Alps in his "Courmyer, North Italy," with breadth and scope.

Yet the city is portrayed with deft touches and in noble and expressive language by C. Myles Collier, in "Along the Canal"; by Edward W. Redfield, in his "Twilight, Paris," and with a rich, golden tone by George Inness, Jr., in a view from his studio window in Paris. All these canvases are pictures of the highest merit.

Indeed there was no picture of the kind like Turner's "Slave ship," for the Royal Academy hanging committee, when it was first exhibited, began by putting it upside down. There was a higher

A VILLAGE STREET, IN THE OLD STAGE DAYS
By E. L. Henry

level over previous years, so that it was apparent that the seventy-sixth annual exhibition of the National Academy of Design afforded much that might please and not a little that might delight the intelligent spectator. To what extent this higher level is to be attributed to the younger men whose works were exhibited might possibly be a debatable question, but certainly the more liberal policy of the Academicians as regards rising artists of merit is to be commended.

DAVID C. PREYER.

RECENT WORK BY DANIEL CHESTER FRENCH

The work of Daniel Chester French stands conspicuous among American sculpture for its manifold excellence, and fortunate the community that can boast the possession of one or more of his masterpieces. His statues are happy in conception and equally happy in execution. His art is of the chaste, dignified, earnest sort that one likes to see in public places—a potent educational influence, a refiner of the masses, a mute inspirer to purer thought and better life.

The new capitol at St. Paul, Minnesota, will have six of his most noteworthy productions of recent years, and the committee having the placing of the commission showed wisdom in the selection of an artist.

No American sculptor has done more or better work than Mr. French.

DANIEL CHESTER FRENCH

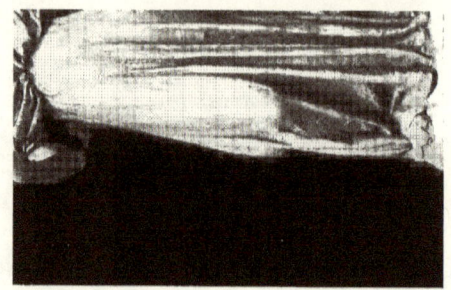
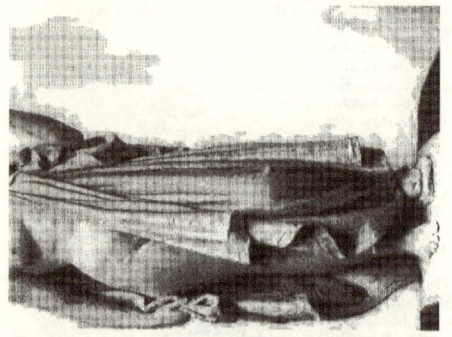

INTEGRITY
By Daniel Chester French
Courtesy of The Architectural Record

COURAGE
By Daniel Chester French
Courtesy of The Architectural Record

He has a genius for plastic art, and that genius has been widely recognized and substantially encouraged. For more than a quarter of a century Mr. French has been honored with many of the most important commissions in the gift of the people, and, unlike many of the favored of fortune, his later works have maintained the promise of his first efforts.

In the long list of his productions, his ideal or symbolic pieces have been perhaps his most beautiful and ennobling creations, and of this class are the six statues for the St. Paul capitol. The main sculptural group of this building will be a bronze quadriga indicative of progress. This will grace the central pavilion over the main entrance, and beneath it, in front of a false attic, will be placed the French statues.

They are symbolized moral qualities, representing respectively Prudence, Truth, Bounty, Integrity, Wisdom, and Courage—the moral qualities to which the state owes its development. Four of the statues, Bounty, Truth, Prudence, and Wisdom, are female figures, and are among the finest the artist has modeled, the first three especially being remarkable for their simplicity and their beauty of face and figure. Wisdom is severer and more conventional, but is yet eminently in keeping with the idea symbolized. Courage finds its exemplification in the figure of a Roman soldier, and Integrity in a toga-draped statesman.

The illustrations given herewith will give some idea of the essential character of the work. The embodiment of an abstract idea gives a wide latitude to an artist, and he is wise who subordinates the merely symbolic to the purely human interest, since it is the natural human interest, and not the conventional symbolism, that impresses the multitude. Mr. French in his figures has for the most part sinned, if one may so express it, on the right side.

Prudence has her lamp, gracefully held near her shoulder; Truth, her mirror reflecting back her own countenance; and Bounty, her sheaf. But these witnesses of symbolism are mere incidental features. What impresses one is the superb figure-work, the chaste beauty of the countenances; in other words, the idealization of the human. Prudence's lamp might be put into Truth's hand, and Truth's mirror into Bounty's. The shifting of symbolism would not be noticed, nor would any one of the figures lose one jot or tittle of its intrinsic interest. They are simply idealized female figures, spiritualized and made instinct with moral quality; and in beholding the superb creations one feels their influence, and is little inclined to seek a label or quibble over the appropriateness of a name.

To most people, probably, Wisdom, with its stiff pose and formal air, will seem the least satisfactory of the six figures. It is suggestive of a Greek carytid. The countenance is majestic, the pose dignified, and the treatment of drapery excellent; but still one misses in it the graceful lines of the other three female figures, and it is not easy to see wherein symbolism gains by the loss of feminine grace.

The male figures, Courage and Integrity, are well conceived and eminently natural. There is no exaggeration, no theatricality in the Roman soldier, nothing of braggadocio or daring. The courage suggested is the courage of conviction, backed by manly resoluteness and quiet determination. And so with Integrity: it is simply a human form indicative of manly qualities, and as such it commands attention and admiration.

The six symbolic figures are fully up to Mr. French's high standard and are to be regarded as among the best examples of architectural statuary produced in recent years.

NELSON R. ABBOTT.

QUADRIGA
By F. W. Ruckstuhl
Pan-American Exposition

ARTISTIC PHOTOGRAPHY
Plate Eleven

BRIDGE IN THE WILDERNESS
By Henry Troth

VENETIAN FISHING-BOAT
By William Schmedigen

THE ARTIST'S QUEST OF TYPES

Convention in modern life is fast robbing the artist classes of their most cherished material. Its thralldom dominates everything. One sees its fell influence in dress, in manners and customs, in home decoration, in the manner in which grounds are laid out and adorned, even in smirks and smiles that are fashioned after the approved pattern. As a rule, the better the appearance a person makes, according to the prevailing notions and canons of taste, the fewer distinctive features he offers worthy of the study of the artist. The smarter or more "improved" an estate is, the less it has to offer in picturesque beauty.

In a word, fashion rules with an iron hand, and from the artist's standpoint, tends to crush out the soul from man and his surroundings. Time was when the artist could say with the positiveness of conviction, "Thou art Peter." Now he looks at his prospective subject and is in doubt. There is something of Peter in him, it is true; not a little of Paul and Luke and John; marked suggestions of the hatter, the clothier, the designer of ties, the inventor of social forms that harness humanity, and other such unmistakable adjuncts of modern make-up. But Peter? His personality is largely gone—vanished with the money he had to pay for his outfit and his social status. He is Peter—plus.

And so with those bits of God's footstool we call "lands reclaimed

WOMAN IN WHITE
By William Schmedtgen

from the wilderness." They are tricked out with a monotony of barbed wire or snake fences and other et ceteras of development. Their fields, gardens, orchards, lanes, cabbage-rows, ricks, everything, savors of geometry. And nobody but Euclid ever thought geometry was artistic.

Civilization, to cut a long story short, while it is the great refiner of mankind, is also the great commoner. It tends to a uniformity of practices and styles; it crushes out individuality; suborns personal tastes. Strong individual types that were once so common as never to provoke a word of comment are now so rare as to suggest the enterprise of coralling them in museums for exhibition purposes. Speaking broadly, gentility is prone, like water, to seek a level, whose placid surface—it is bad form for gentility to be disturbed—scarcely offers a ripple or an artistic white cap to break tiresome sameness.

To be sure, there are still expressive eyes, strong noses, shapely chins, lordly carriages. But, goodness, trousers are all shaped on the same pattern and hung in the same way; coats are cut variously, but worn according to rule; hats, ditto. An unwritten law divorces the silk hat from the sack-coat—and everybody knows a sack-coat and a silk hat make a picturesque combination!

And women's attire—well, it's the same thing over again. We have balloon sleeves one season and skin-tight arm-coverings the next; golf-skirts to-day and street-sweeping trains to-morrow; reds for all complexions this season and electric blues

and bronze greens for another. To-day the modiste recognizes that nature knows a thing or two about anatomy. To-morrow she changes her mind, and invents some warping, squeezing, or otherwise distorting device, into whose shaping-mold she undertakes to run all feminine humanity. As a natural result, types vanish into a more or less uniform style of display figures for the costume-maker, the dictator of manners, the prescriber of social proprieties.

And the artist? He is obliged, unless he be content to be commissioned to paint the animated lay-figures just mentioned, to search long and earnestly for his types, and to be satisfied with those odds and ends of humanity whom fashion has not found, or whom untoward fortune has made resigned to outfits in keeping with their personalities and their purses.

MOOR WITH SNUFF-BOX
By William Schmedigen

This is not meant to be jocular. It is a strict statement of fact. The artist to-day must seek his strong types among the lower, less ambitious, and less progressive classes in his own country, or go abroad, where the centuries might get mixed up by mistake, and in the absence of pointers in the way of changed manners and habiliments, one would never know the difference. In the middle and upper classes, where Dame Fashion, Mrs. Grundy, and their equally autocratic male associates hold sway, the tendency is to merge all types into one composite type, permitting only such slight variations as are necessary for the identification of names.

The art student takes a long course of instruction at some institution; perhaps he goes abroad and "studies under the best masters." He works assiduously days or months limning the divine proportions of the Apollo Belvedere or of the Venus de Milo; he becomes so engrossed with his subjects that their graces become his dreams. He studies artistic anatomy and familiarizes himself with the mystery of expression. He conceives the idea of painting a legion, more or less, of distinct types—limbs supple, carriages free and natural, faces strong with character and marked with the impress of individuality; then he advertises or goes out on the street to look for what he has been dreaming about, and he finds a comparatively characterless multitude.

RETURNING SCOUT
By William Schmedtgen

Charles Lamb divided mankind into two classes—those who borrow and those who lend. The artist, after a few weeks' search, is led to believe that Lamb wrote with a personal bias. He is inclined to make a new classification—the overwhelming majority who follow convention, and the inconspicuous minority who are so disloyal to the spirit of civilization, albeit loyal to themselves, as to snap their fingers at convention and be brave enough to own themselves simply Peters or Marys without borrowed trimmings.

It is a notable fact that a large percentage of the artists who have attained distinction as painters or sketch artists of character have gone to fields where human life is simple, or robust, or possibly degraded. Once in a while, to be sure, one will find a Charles Dana Gibson who has made a hit with society's lay-figures and given the world fashion-plates whose charm is a certain conventional grace and beauty. But these fashion-plates cannot by the grossest license of statement be called types. Delsarte, Worth & Company, and their predecessors in the same line of business, killed the type features in this class of people long ago.

The artist to-day has to go on the byways rather than on the boulevards of life to find what he wants.

This is practically what workers in other lines have had to do. Cable found his types among the Creoles; Charles Egbert Craddock, in the Tennessee mountains; Bret Harte, among the western camps; Joel Chandler Harris, in the negro cabins; Dickens, in London's byways. There they found types of character, untouched by the refining, leveling, obliterating finger of civilization, that were acceptable to the multitude from their very novelty. Remington and some other artists have acquired a vogue by the same practice; and the

TYPICAL CUBAN
By William Schmedigen

more unique the types, the more they have been stamped with a strong individuality dissimilar from what one finds in reception-rooms and parquets, the more acceptable have been the pictures.

The artist who would find types in his own city had better shun the genteel emporiums, where one customer is a fairly correct trans-

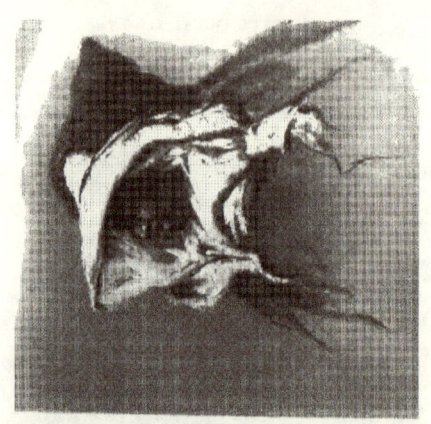
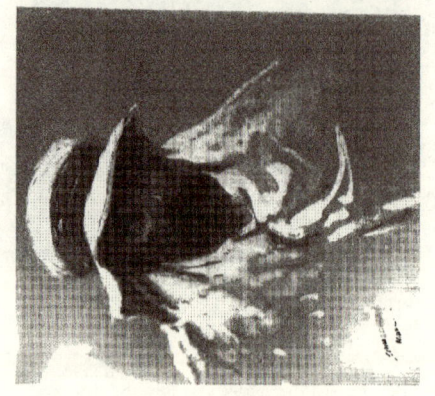

cript of another, and visit the bargain stores, where the pinch of circumstances has left its impress upon the patrons' faces, and one can see the value of a dollar expressed in eager glances, and chapters of past experience written in wrinkles or expressed in terms of self-aggression.

All this is preliminary, but to the point. It serves to explain why so many artists make pilgrimages to the semi-dead communities of the Old World in search of unique characters. It is the comparative dearth at home of types acceptable to the artist—and to the purchasers of the finished pictures—that led William Schmedtgen, whose studies illustrate this article, to visit Cuba, and thence cross the Atlantic to Morocco, southern Spain and Italy, to sojourn in these countries in quest of costumes and faces that have not been drawn or painted *ad nauseam.*

The essential characteristics desired were strangeness or strength of features, individuality of dress — something indicative of a life sharply removed from that of the progressive, up-to-date communities one usually finds in this country. The pictures speak for themselves. The types caught are foreign to what

BIT OF COLOR IN VENICE
By William Schmedtgen

one meets in ordinary intercourse, and have, therefore, an unusual interest and value.

Had the Cubans portrayed been accustomed to balance dishes on their hands and look for a tip with the finger-bowl, their types would have been different. Had these rugged-looking old Moors been wont to wear Rogers, Peet & Co.'s ready-made clothes and conform to the fashion of starched shirts and stand-up collars, their countenances would doubtless betray the fact.

In many of the small towns of the Old World life is stagnant. With certain limitations, the individual preferences of the rank and file take the place of fashions. Provincial as the people are, they are ultra-metropolitan in their indifference as to their own or other people's appearance. They have their own notions, are circumscribed by their own conditions, and they dress accordingly, oblivious to the fact, or perhaps glorying in the fact, that they are different from their neighbors.

MOORISH MERCHANT
By William Schmedigen

As the caravans come into the markets of Morocco, for instance, one may see an assemblage of five hundred or more Moors, and no two dressed alike. In such a gathering, there is brilliancy of coloring, life, animation—anything but the dapper sleekness or frayed gentility of dress observable where fashion rules and manufacturing enterprise makes one man the reflex of another. In the fish-markets of Italy, again, there is the same indifference to convention and the same sturdy reliance on self. The people are untouched by court or court manners, and each, as regards appearance, is a law unto himself. Even the children are individual in the uniqueness and picturesqueness of their dress.

As might naturally be expected under such conditions, the artist finds a wider range of strong facial characteristics than at home. The great commoner that has done so much to soften and refine the features in more civilized communities has there made little progress. The seaports of northern Africa and the coast towns of Italy and Spain are, therefore, in a sense, an artist's paradise as regards picturesque types. They have virtually remained untouched for centuries by the influences that abound in more progressive communities, and they will doubtless remain so for centuries to come. Every Moor, every Italian fisherman, every toiler of southern Spain is Peter, not Peter minus what convention has taken from him. In this country one would scarcely dare to follow the license of individual preference that is common in these Old-World communities, and hence the artist will rarely find here characters betraying in their bearing and in their every lineament such marked evidences of free, untrammeled individual life.

Strong personal traits, such as the artist prizes, be they in looks, in dress, or in customs, are fostered in communities which civilization has barely reached, or which are indifferent to progress, advancement, and general social culture. Semi-barbarous races and such out of the way nooks and corners as were visited by Mr. Schmedtgen thus offer a seductive field for research. The painter is taken away from the realm of shop-made men and modiste-made women, and is led into the land of the non-conformists. An Arab trader on the desert or a fishwife in an Italian seaport is not accustomed to conform to much of anything, and hence their value as types. It is an old maxim that, intellectually, the world's heretics are its most interest-

AN ARAB
By William Schmedtgen

ing personages. And, in a sense, the residents of these out of the way places are the heretics of convention.

A couple of years ago colored pictures of Indians were the fad, and hundreds of thousands of them found ready sale. It was not that they were especially beautiful: they were simply types of faces and costumes that took people away from the dress-by-rule and act-by-precept walks of modern life. The Indians have had their day; the negroes, the denizens of the slums, and other such characters have been well worked. One can scarcely blame the artist for his exploring proclivities.

ELLIS T. CLARKE.

AT EL PASO
By William Schmedigen

MOURNING HER BRAVE
By J. H. Sharp

AMERICAN PAINTINGS
Plate Eleven

NOTABLE WESTERN EXHIBITIONS

One of the most commendable enterprises of the Chicago Art Institute — and it is a feature of the management that might well serve as an inspiration to other similar institutions — is the provision it makes for varied and comprehensive exhibitions of high-class art works. These exhibitions range from collections of paintings by aspirants, who are thus given an introduction to the public, to loan exhibitions of the works of masters, that are often brought together at no inconsiderable cost and trouble, for the purpose of giving students and picture lovers the privilege of enjoying what, under ordinary circumstances, would be barred to them.

Recently, in addition to displaying the works of Chicago artists as a body, and of various painters as individuals, the Institute had a magnificent exhibition of selected works of modern masters, that were generously loaned by their owners for the occasion. And during the last month the institution has given no less than five exhibitions. Three of these were one-man shows, being the work of Joseph Lindon Smith, William Otis Swett, Jr., and P. A. Dagnan-Bouveret. The other two were the fifth annual exhibition of the Society of Western Artists and the exhibition of the Country Sketch Club of New York.

Naturally, interest largely centered on the paintings of the famous Frenchman, who is admittedly one of the greatest, if not the greatest, of living painters of religious subjects. The collection offered by the Institute comprised only twenty-nine subjects, but it was fairly representative of Dagnan's best work. It showed at once his strength and his weakness, his wonderful power of infusing his own deep religious nature, his spirituality and devotion, into his creations, and his proneness, especially in his more pretentious religious pictures, to yield to the conventional, the artificial, and even the theatrical.

His painting, "The Disciples at Emmaus," loaned by the Carnegie Art Gallery at Pittsburg, was given, as perhaps it deserved, the place of honor. It is a formal composition, as correct in drawing as might be expected from such a master as Dagnan, and suffused with a rich glow that bespeaks the colorist. And yet, withal, it is a picture so hazardous in its conception as to be unconvincing. Some of his simpler canvases, one is inclined to think, afford greater evidences of his ability as an artist. His "Benediction," for instance, in which a peasant bestows his blessing upon a newly married couple, and his pictures of horse-troughs and of simple

Breton scenes, are instinct with a naturalness and vigor one misses in his more studied and elaborate religious scenes.

The exhibition was one of the best ever given in this country of the work of this eminent artist, and all praise is due to the Institute for gathering examples of his work from such diverse sources and offering them to the public.

The fifth annual exhibition of the Society of Western Artists, comprising over a hundred pictures, was one of varied excellence. Frank Duveneck's large marine, a well-studied and effective piece of painting, was one of the best pictures of the collection. J. H. Sharp's "Mourning Her Brave," reproduced herewith, is an unconventional subject powerfully treated and a canvas of commanding interest. It is a picture from the life, and for that reason has a force and strength not usually inherent in fanciful creations. Bert Phillips's three Indian heads, Charles Partridge Adams's brilliant sunset, Pauline Dohn's "The Seeker," a musing woman under an apple-tree, L. H. Meakin's landscapes, J. Ottis Adams's "Indiana Highlands," and T. C. Steele's "On Mount Carmel Pike" should be mentioned as among the best canvases displayed.

The exhibition of the New York Country Sketch Club was for the most part the work of men whose names are comparatively unfamiliar to the public. The display gave evidence of freshness and spontaneity, but was marked by an amateurishness suggestive of large possibilities in the way of improvement. Joseph Lindon Smith, in his faithful depictions of the work of old masters, has ventured on comparatively untrodden paths, and it must be said, with marvelous success. His painted sculpture, bronze figures, and architectural details are so well done as to be worthy of extended study. William Otis Swett's twenty-odd canvases were low-toned and somber, being largely depictions of evening and night effects. The spectator would gladly have welcomed an occasional touch of light and sunshine; but was forced to admit that the paintings were a marked improvement, both in conception and in execution, over the artist's earlier performances. C. A. HARRIS.

ST. JOHN
By S. Cecilia Cotter

BRUSH AND PENCIL

Vol. VIII　　　　　MAY, 1901　　　　　No. 2

PHILADELPHIA WATER-COLOR EXHIBITION

The private viewing of the most recent aquarelle show on April 5th proved to be wholesome, interesting, and pregnant with many first-class interpolations.

The *tout ensemble*, embracing some three hundred and fifty numbers, would from the layman's standpoint be declared charming; from the artist's view, however, the measure of praise is identified with three adjectives—good, toneful, and interesting.

From an independent corner, it may be said that the collection proves on analysis to be a series of good qualities well expressed, and honest in execution, subjects and locations chosen, perhaps, with a desire to catch the public eye, and so adapted with the aid of a well-filled palette as to be synonymous with truthful, sober art, standing aloof from any drum-beating or snapshot smokeless explosions. It takes up rather the attitude of the well-read traveler, who disdains the use of an atlas to point out in his extended line of geographical argument the topography of a country. He indicates it with a wave of the hand, and warms up with enthusiasm as to the pleasant or noxious characteristic of that pre-empted location.

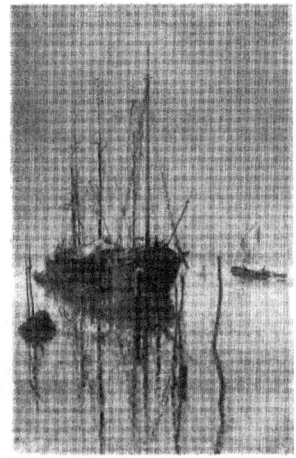

SEAFARERS
By John Wesley Little

The main gallery, in order to give space to the many exhibits, has been divided into three rooms, wherein you may view the pictorial

SURF AT CUSHING'S ISLAND
By George Howell Gay

construction, well bolstered or cemented, and it please ye better, as—I am choosing them indiscriminately—Thomas B. Craig, Harry Eaton, Thomas and Peter Moran, Carlton T. Chapman, Melbourne Hardwick, Walter T. Palmer, C. Morgan McIllhenny, C. Myles Collier, J. G. Brown, F. K. M. Rehn, Childe Hassam, H. Bolton-Jones, Stephen J. Ferris, F. Ballard Williams, W. Granville Smith, James B. Sword, Carl Weber, Frank English, and I raise my hat in deference to the two opalescent contributions of Mrs. J. Francis Murphy.

No. 295, "Coming from the Spring," is a softly modulated hymn of praise, with a musical rhythm, low in cadence, sweet in expression; a fit companion to "A Frosty Morning," wherein the silent hills beyond stand but as sentinels to bar the incursion of Jack Frost upon the suggested ravine and chirping rill of water trickling in the foreground mist. Simple, unaffected, low in key, it stands as a symphony of gray with a slight indication of a silver fume in the cloud-land beyond.

Sturdy, direct, with a full and vigorous harmony, "The Oak," by F. Ballard Williams, has been accorded a position of honor —the main center of the main gallery. The virile handling of mass and line, the low-tone treatment of even the upper notes, and the fulsome, luminous sky will set the juniors wondering, and smaller patrons wild with envy.

THE OAK
By Fred B. Williams

An inspection of the two cattle pieces, "Cattle on the Shore," by Thomas Craig, and "The Woodland Pool," by Peter Moran, notwithstanding its execrable placing, leaves the palm of favor decidedly in the hands of the latter. Both in drawing and handling of the color, motion and anatomy, Moran has exerted himself to an attainment with a very enviable result. The "Two Friends," calves though they be, is a nice adjustment of light and shade, with a strong indication of good drawing and a subtle handling of the medium vehicles of color.

The illustrator's art is identified in the forcible expressions of black-and-white at the hands of George Gibbs, to wit: "A Flogging in the British Navy," "Captain Hull on the Constitution," and "A Surprise in the Cabin."

Among the landscapists there looms up the soft, marshy foregrounds and woodlands of Henry Farrer, "When Autumn Woods are Waning," "The Twilight's Thoughtful Hour," and "Sunset"; and near by in direct contradistinction is the pristine green of Harry Eaton's "Pond," that little bend or elbow of the stream that gave him the gold medal at the last fall exhibition.

STUDY OF A FRENCH PEASANT
By Clara D. Davidson

Challenging, however, those who would dare to insinuate his inability to paint in other than this virginal green, turn, and you will find on the screen opposite a nice composition bearing the legend, "Russet and Brown." It is among these that one finds the special degrees of generalization.

Speaking of snow reminds one that Walter Palmer's array is in bad company. His three contributions are wedged in between others bearing deeper and more somber tones, consequently making them appear thin and scarce up to the standard of his past efforts.

In figure-work the head and shoulders of a "Clytie," by A. M. Turner, is a highly commendable piece of work, both in the lines of anatomy and of coloring, the only point of condemnation being the injudicious framing and the absence of a mat. This is a source of real regret, since the treatment of the subject affords the utmost satisfaction and wins loud praise from many of the gray-beards. Companions on the right, "Katherine," a pastel by E. Plaisted Abbot, and "The Witch," by Paul Jones, are worthy of more than passing notice.

THE BEGGAR MAID
By H. T. Cariss

From Leon Moran, three parts in essence pretty, might as usual be bestowed on 310 and 314, depicting the lady and gentleman of the eighteenth century. A new departure is acceptable. The use of the French gray paper condones the measures of the brighter tints.

Apropos, however, sturdy Thomas Moran is a near neighbor with his "Morning in Arizona" and "The Cliffs of Green River, Wyoming," and I think me there is no better exponent of God's own architecture. From the base to the pinnacle the volcanic upheaval and descendant stand in sullenness and pride, dignified and morose, yielding nothing but a diversified quality and quantity, unintelligible, unconquered, but brought nearer home by Mr. Moran than by any other artist throughout the length and breadth of the land.

To Alexander Schilling the Art Club gold medal, for "Upland Fields," has been awarded by the committee, composed of George Gibbs, chairman; Dr. Charles W. Kessler, David Wilson Jordan,

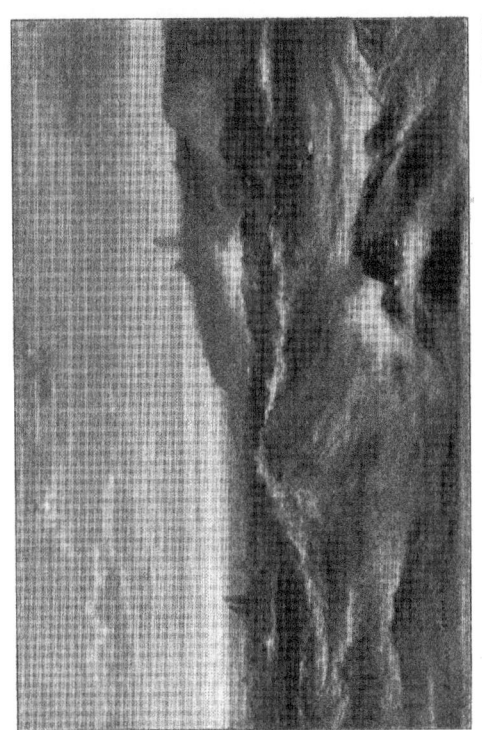
BAY OF FUNDY
By Edward Moran

Joseph S. Kennard, and Charles F. Ziegler. But why? Does any one know? In solemn truth it is but a 16 by 20, showing a dull rising upland and a flat leaden sky, bereft of art or elegance. "The Oak," by Williams, or Anshutz's well-modeled pastel of Dr. Davis, bearing the legend of "The Cello Player," would but too

CATTLE ON THE SHORE
By Thomas B. Craig

surely have given better satisfaction, since this latter is a sterling bit of work vigorously drawn, suggestive of action, nice in poise or balance, and well attuned.

J. B. Sword, following in the line of his success of 1897, again exhibits a vessel bearing down in the "Morning Mists." In this he displays his forte in the depth and liquid qualities of the water. A radical departure may be witnessed in "The End of the Holidays," a pleasing composition, excellent in tone, portraying a street swept by a blizzard against which man and beast struggle with every sense of aggressive action. "Prisoners to the Rear" is an excellent composition by R. F. Zogbaum, carrying our thoughts back to 1862-63 when the tide of battle score and victory was turning in favor of the North.

For exquisite transparent chrome effect in water and sky, a small contribution by F. K. M. Rehn, catalogued as "Morning on the

WINTER ALONG EAST RIVER
By Carlton T. Chapman

New Jersey Coast," is without a rival among the marines. As an evidence of its general favor *ipso facto*, it found a purchaser before the smoker was half-way through, and left two very disappointed aspirants for its possession. Yet this little poetical expression is but 14 by 18, a newly born sun rising in a flood of golden sheen tinging the incoming waves as they roll on a gold sun-riched beach.

It is but a resurgam, and I shall hail with delight when Melbourne H. Hardwick seeks a new land and other men and women. "The North Sea" is threadbare, and one becomes very tired of looking upon that same old brown-sailed lugger and those self-same fishermen and women, honest though they be.

J. L. Gerome Ferris is identified with an ambitious Moorish figure of a girl with a soft-coated gazelle as her companion; a fine color scheme, with a background of nicely executed detail of Moorish architecture. H. T. Cariss, listed with three, is seen at his best in "Down by the Old Spring House," an old-fashioned song, but well sung.

Fred Pitts, Louis F. Faber, Frank English, Carl Weber, Harrington Fitzgerald, Franz Lesshafft, E. Taylor Snow, all deserve mention for the splendid efforts made.

To Miss Evelyn Heysinger, as an earnest of her endeavor, I trust to see more of her work. "Walnut Street Theater on a Rainy Night" is well and aptly expressed. Laura E. Snow's "Sandy Run Meadows, N. J.," shows marked ability and good perceptive qualities; and "Summer," by Marianna Sloan, is a subject one might always live with.

"The Arrival of a Liner," by E. M. Bicknell, is big, broad, and full of motion. The big bows loom up in tow of two perky little tugboats, and one awaits the shrill whistle to give the finishing touch to a scene realistic. "A Group of the Queen's Royal Stag-Hounds," by R. H. Poore, while acceptable as a good piece of work, is unfortunately lacking the sense of originality. Nevertheless it finds a resting-place and a home in the precincts of the club.

W. P. LOCKINGTON.

RECENT WORK OF ILLUSTRATORS—JOSEPH PENNELL

Joseph Pennell needs no introduction to the American public. His illustrations, strongly individual and beautifully executed, have long been regarded as among the finest specimens of this particular form of art. His book work, however, is not as widely known as that which he has done for the magazines, and the following examples will therefore be acceptable to the reader:

NANTES
By Joseph Pennell
From "A Little Tour in France"
Copyright, 1900, Houghton, Mifflin & Co.

BORDEAUX, THE QUAYS
By Joseph Pennell
From "A Little Tour in France"
Copyright, 1900, Houghton, Mifflin & Co.

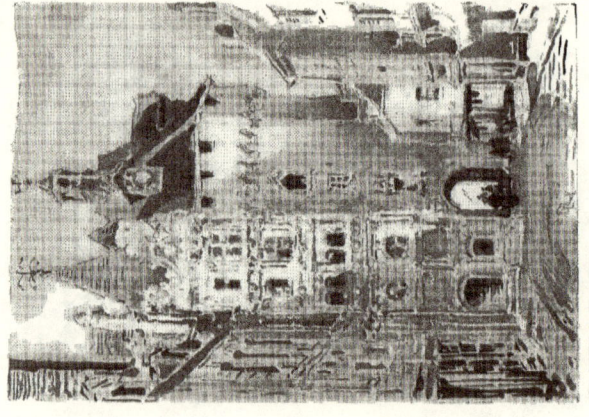

OLD TOWN GATE, LOCHES
By Joseph Pennell
From "A Little Tour in France"
Copyright, 1900, Houghton, Mifflin & Co.

LANGEAIS
By Joseph Pennell
From "A Little Tour in France"
Copyright, 1900, Houghton, Mifflin & Co.

CHAUMONT, FROM THE LOIRE
By Joseph Pennell
From "A Little Tour in France"
Copyright, 1900, Houghton, Mifflin & Co.

BLOIS, FROM THE LOIRE
By Joseph Pennell
From "A Little Tour in France"
Copyright, 1900, Houghton, Mifflin & Co.

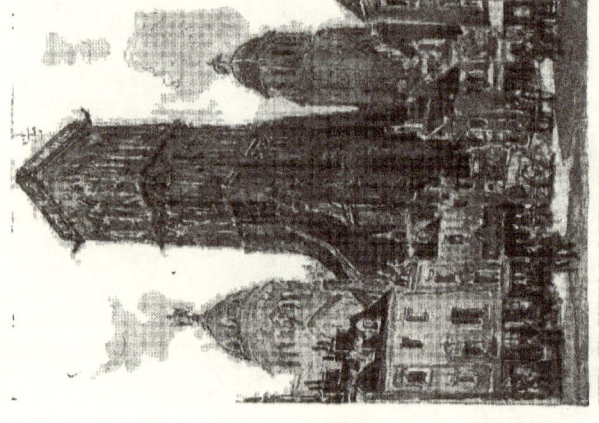

TOURS, THE TOWERS OF SAINT MARTIN
By Joseph Pennell
From "A Little Tour in France"
Copyright, 1900, Houghton, Mifflin & Co.

OLD TIMBERED HOUSES, ANGERS
By Joseph Pennell
From "A Little Tour in France"
Copyright, 1900, Houghton, Mifflin & Co.

THE ART AND CRAFT OF THE MACHINE *

As we work along our various ways, there takes shape within us, in some sort, an ideal—something we are to become—some work to be done. This, I think, is denied to very few, and we begin really to live only when the thrill of this ideality moves us in what we will to accomplish.

In the years which have been devoted in my own life to working out in stubborn materials a feeling for the beautiful, in the vortex of distorted complex conditions, a hope has grown stronger with the experience of each year, amounting now to a gradually deepening conviction, that in the machine lies the only future of art and craft—as I believe, a glorious future; that the machine is, in fact, the metamorphosis of ancient art and craft; that we are at last face to face with the machine—the modern Sphinx—whose riddle the artist must solve if he would that art live—for his nature holds the key.

The great ethics of the machine are as yet, in the main, beyond the ken of the artist or student of sociology; but the artist mind may now approach the nature of this thing from experience, which has become the commonplace of his field, to suggest, in time, I hope, to prove, that the machine is capable of carrying to fruition high ideals in art—higher than the world has yet seen!

Disciples of William Morris cling to an opposite view. Yet William Morris himself deeply sensed the danger to art of the transforming force whose sign and symbol is the thing of brass and steel we familiarly call a machine, and though of the new art we eagerly seek he sometimes despaired, he quickly renewed his hope. He plainly foresaw that a blank in fine art would follow the inevitable abuse of new-found power, and threw himself body and soul into the work of bridging it over by bringing into our lives afresh the beauty of art as she had been, that the new art to come might not have dropped too many stitches nor have unraveled what would still be useful to her. That he had abundant faith in the new art his every essay will testify. That he miscalculated the machine does not matter. He did sublime work for it when he pleaded so well for the process of elimination its abuse had made necessary; when he fought the innate vulgarity of theocratic impulse in art as opposed to democratic; and when he preached the gospel of simplicity.

All artists love and honor William Morris. He did the best in his time for art, and will live in history as the great socialist, together

* Copyright, 1901, by the Chicago Architectural Club. Abridged from an address published in the Club's Catalogue and reprinted in BRUSH AND PENCIL by special permission.

with Ruskin, the great moralist: a significant fact worth thinking about, that the two great reformers of modern times professed the artist. The machine these reformers protested, because the sort of luxury which is born of greed had usurped it and made of it a terrible engine of enslavement, deluging the civilized world with a murderous ubiquity, which plainly enough was the damnation of their art and craft. It had not then advanced to the point which now so plainly indicates that it will surely and swiftly, by its own momentum, undo the mischief it has made, and the usurping vulgarians as well. Nor was it so grown as to become apparent to William Morris, the grand democrat, that the machine was the great forerunner of democracy. The ground plan of this thing is now grown to the point where the artist must take it up no longer as a protest: genius must progressively dominate the work of the contrivance it has created; to lend a useful hand in building afresh the "Fairness of the Earth."

That the machine has dealt art in the grand old sense a death-blow, none will deny. The evidence is too substantial. Art in the grand old sense—meaning art in the sense of structural tradition, whose craft is fashioned upon the handicraft ideal, ancient or modern; an art wherein this form and that form as structural parts were laboriously joined in such a way as beautifully to emphasize the manner of the joining: the million and one ways of beautifully satisfying bare structural necessities, which have come down to us chiefly through the books as "art."

For the purpose of suggesting hastily, and therefore crudely, wherein the machine has sapped the vitality of this art, let us assume architecture in the old sense as a fitting representative of traditional art, and printing as a fitting representation of the machine. What printing—the machine—has done for architecture—the fine art—will have been done in measure of time for all art immediately fashioned upon the early handicraft ideal.

With a masterful hand Victor Hugo, a lover and a great student of architecture, traces her fall in "Notre Dame." The prophecy of Frollo, that "The book will kill the edifice," I remember was to me as a boy one of the sad things of the world. After seeking the origin and tracing the growth of architecture in superb fashion, showing how in the middle ages all the intellectual forces of the people converged to one point—architecture—he shows how, in the life of that time, whoever was born poet became an architect. All other arts simply obeyed and placed themselves under the discipline of architecture. They were the workmen of the great work. The architect, the poet, the master, summed up in his person the sculpture which carved his façades, the painting which illuminated his walls and windows, the music which set his bells to pealing and breathed into his organs—there was nothing which was not forced in order to make something of itself in that time, to come and frame itself in the edifice.

Thus down to the time of Gutenberg architecture is the principal writing—the universal writing of humanity. In the fifteenth century everything changes. Human thought discovers a mode of perpetuating itself, not only more resisting than architecture, but still more simple and easy. Architecture is dethroned. The book is about to kill the edifice.

See how architecture now withers away, how little by little it becomes lifeless and bare. How one feels the water sinking, the sap departing, the thought of the times and people withdrawing from it. The chill is almost imperceptible in the fifteenth century the press is yet weak, and at most draws from architecture a superabundance of life, but with the beginning of the sixteenth century, the malady of architecture is visible. It becomes classic art in a miserable manner; from being indigenous, it becomes Greek and Roman; from being true and modern, it becomes pseudo-classic. It is this decadence which we call the Renaissance. It is the setting sun which we mistake for dawn. It has now no power to hold the other arts; so they emancipate themselves, break the yoke of the architect, and take themselves off, each in its own direction. Sculpture becomes statuary, the image trade becomes painting, the canon becomes music. Hence Raphael, Angelo, and those splendors of the dazzling sixteenth century.

Meanwhile, what becomes of printing? All the life, leaving architecture, comes to it. In proportion as architecture ebbs and flows, printing swells and grows. That capital of forces which human thought had been expending in building is hereafter to be expended in books; and architecture, as it was, is dead, irretrievably slain by the printed book. Thenceforth, if architecture rise again, reconstruct, as Hugo prophesies she may begin to do in the latter days of the nineteenth century, she will no longer be mistress, she will be one of the arts, never again *the* art.

So the organic process, of which the majestic decline of architecture is only one case in point, has steadily gone on down to the present time, and still goes on, weakening the hold of the artist upon the people, drawing off from his rank poets and scientists until architecture is but a little, poor knowledge of archeology, and the average of art is reduced to the gasping poverty of imitative realism; until the whole letter of tradition, the vast fabric of precedent, in the flesh, which has increasingly confused the art ideal while the machine has been growing to power, is a beautiful corpse from which the spirit has flown.

So the artist craft wanes. And, invincible, triumphant, the machine goes on, gathering force and knitting the material necessities of mankind ever closer into a universal automatic fabric, the works of art of the century!

The machine is intellect mastering the drudgery of earth that the plastic art may live; that the margin of leisure and strength by which man's life upon the earth can be made beautiful, may immeasurably widen; its function ultimately to emancipate human expression! It is a universal educator, surely raising the level of human intelligence, so carrying within itself the power to destroy, by its own momentum, the greed which in Morris's time and still in our own time turns it to a deadly engine of enslavement. The only comfort left the poor artist, side-tracked as he is, seemingly is a mean one: the thought that the very selfishness which man's early art idealized, now reduced to its lowest terms, is swiftly and surely destroying itself through the medium of the machine.

The artist's present plight is a sad one, but may he truthfully say that society is less well off because architecture, or even art, as it was, is dead, and printing, or the machine, lives? Is it not more likely that the medium of artistic expression itself has broadened and changed until a new definition and new direction must be given the art activity of the future, and that the machine has finally made for the artist, whether he will yet own it or not, a splendid distinction between the art of old and the art to come?

To shed some light upon this distinction, let us take an instance in the field naturally ripened first by the machine—the commercial field. The tall modern office building is the machine pure and simple. We may here sense an advanced stage of a condition surely entering all art for all time; its already triumphant glare in the deadly struggle taking place here between the machine and the art of structural tradition reveals "art" torn and hung upon the steel frame of commerce, a forlorn head upon a pike, a solemn warning to architects and artists the world over.

We must walk blindfolded not to see that all that this magnificent resource of machine and material has brought us so far is a complete degradation of every type and form sacred to the art of old; a pandemonium of tin masks, huddled deformities, and decayed methods; quarreling, lying, and cheating. None of the people who do these things, who pay for them or use them, know what they mean, feeling only—when they feel at all—that what is most truly like the past is the safest and therefore the best.

A pitiful insult, art and craft! With this mine of industrial wealth at our feet have we no power to use it except to the perversion of our natural resources? A confession of shame which the merciful ignorance of the yet material frame of things mistakes for glorious achievement.

We half believe in our artistic greatness ourselves when we toss up a pantheon to the god of money in a night or two, or pile up a mammoth aggregation of Roman monuments, sarcophagi, and Greek temples for a postoffice in a year or two—the patient retinue of the machine pitching in with terrible effectiveness to consummate this

PROPOSED PERISTYLE AND ARCH AT THE FOOT OF MARKET STREET, SAN FRANCISCO
Willis Polk, Architect
See article, "Work of the Younger Architects"

unhallowed ambition—this insult to ancient gods. The delicate impressionable facilities of terra-cotta become imitative blocks and voussoirs of tool-marked stone, are badgered into all manner of structural gymnastics, or else ignored in vain endeavor to be honest; and granite blocks, cut in the fashion of the followers of Phidias, are cunningly arranged about the steel beams and shafts, to look "real"—leaning heavily upon an inner skeleton of steel for support from floor to floor, which strains beneath the "reality."

See now, how an element—the vanguard of the new art—has entered here. This element is the structural necessity reduced to a skeleton, complete in itself without the craftsman's touch. At once the million and one little ways of satisfying this necessity beautifully, coming to us chiefly through the books as the traditional art of building, vanish away—become history. The artist is emancipated to work his will with a rational freedom unknown to the laborious art of structural tradition—no longer tied to the meager unit of brick arch and stone lintel, nor hampered by the grammatical phrase of their making. But he cannot use his freedom. His tradition cannot think. He will not think. His scientific brother has put it to him before he is ready.

The art of old idealized a structural necessity—now rendered obsolete and unnatural by the machine—and accomplished it through man's joy in the labor of his hands. The new will weave for the necessity of mankind, which his machine will have mastered, a robe of the ideal no less truthful, but more poetical, with a rational freedom made possible by the machine, beside which the art of old will be as the sweet, plaintive wail of the pipe to the outpouring of full orchestra. It will clothe necessity with the living flesh of virile imagination.

This distinction is one to be felt now rather than clearly defined. The definition is the poetry of this machine age, and will be written large in time; but the more we, as artists, examine into this premonition, the more we will find the utter helplessness of old forms to satisfy new conditions, and the crying need of the machine for plastic treatment—a pliant, sympathetic treatment of its needs that the body of structural precedent cannot yield.

To gain further suggestive evidence of this, let us turn to the decorative arts—the immense middle-ground of all art now mortally sickened by the machine. Here we find the most deadly perversion of all. Without regard to first principles or common decency, the whole letter of tradition—that is, ways of doing things rendered wholly obsolete and unnatural by the machine—is recklessly fed into its rapacious maw until you may buy reproductions for ninety-nine cents of that which originally cost ages of toil and cultivation, reproductions worth intrinsically nothing—harmful parasites befogging the sensibilities of our natures, belittling and falsifying any true perception of normal beauty. the Creator may have seen fit to implant in us.

The idea of fitness to purpose, harmony between form and use with regard to any of these things, is possessed by very few, and utilized by them as a protest chiefly—a protest against the machine! But the machine is the creature and not the creator of iniquity; the machine has noble possibilities unwillingly forced to degradation in the name of the artistic; the machine, as far as its artistic capacity is concerned, is itself the crazed victim of the artist who works while he waits, and the artist who waits while he works.

They are artists clinging sadly to the old order, and would wheedle the giant frame of things back to its childhood or forward to its second childhood, while this machine age is suffering for the artist who accepts, works, and sings as he works, with the joy of the *here* and *now!* We want the man who eagerly seeks and finds, or blames himself if he fails to find, the beauty of this time. Artists who feel toward modernity and the machine now as William Morris and Ruskin were once justified in feeling, had better wait and work sociologically where great work may still be done by them. In the field of art activity they will do distinct harm. Already they have wrought much mischief.

If the artist will only open his eyes he will see that the machine he dreads has made it possible to wipe out the mass of meaningless torture to which mankind, in the name of the artistic, has been more or less subjected since time began; for that matter, has made possible a cleanly strength, an ideality and a poetic fire that the art of the world has not yet seen; for the minions of the machine now smooth away the necessity for petty structural deceits, soothe this wearisome struggle to make things seem what they are not, and can never be; satisfy the simple term of the modern art equation as the ball of clay in the sculptor's hand yields to his desire—comforting forever this realistic, brain-sick masquerade we are wont to suppose art.

William Morris pleaded well for simplicity as the basis of all true art. Let us understand the significance to art of that word—simplicity—for it is vital to the art of the machine. We may find, in place of the genuine thing we have striven for, an affectation of the naïve, which we should detest, as we detest a full-grown woman with baby mannerisms. English art is saturated with it, from the brand-new imitation of the old house that grew and rambled from period to period to the rain-tub standing beneath the eaves. In fact, most simplicity following the doctrines of William Morris is a protest; as a protest, well enough; but the highest form of simplicity is not simple in the sense that the infant intelligence is simple.

Simplicity in art, rightly understood, is a synthetic, positive quality, in which we may see evidence of mind, breadth of scheme, wealth of detail, and withal the sense of completeness found in a tree or a flower. A work may have the delicacies of a rare orchid or the

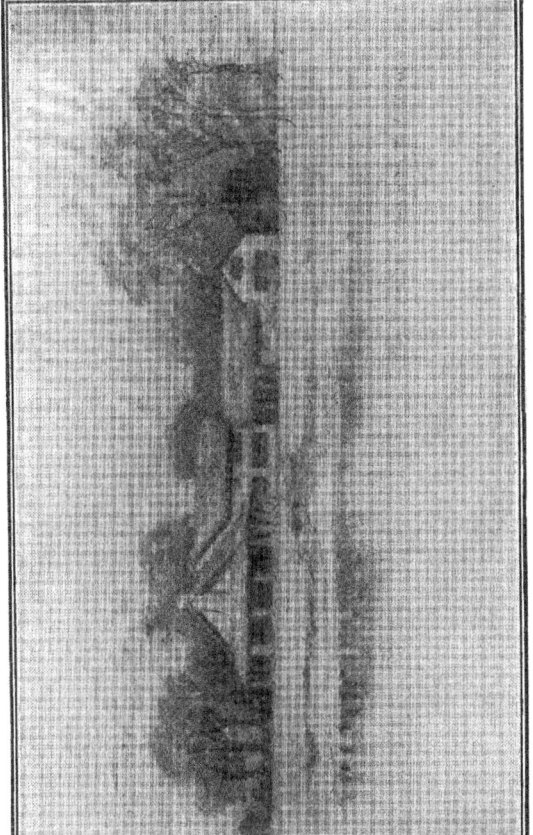

THE RIVER FRONT OF HOUSE FOR MR. EDWARD BRADLEY
Elmer Grey, Architect
See article, "Work of the Younger Architects."

stanch fortitude of the oak, and still be simple. A thing to be simple needs only to be true to itself in organic sense.

With this ideal of simplicity, let us glance hastily at several examples of the machine and see how it has been forced by false ideals to do violence to this simplicity; how it has made possible the highest simplicity, rightly understood and so used. Machinery has been invented for no other purpose than to imitate, as closely as possible, the sentimental forms and the wood-carving of the early ideal—with the immediate result that no ninety-nine-cent piece of furniture is salable without some horrible botchwork meaning nothing unless it means that art and craft have combined to fix in the mind of the masses the old hand-carved product as the *ne plus ultra* of the ideal. Thus is the wood-working industry glutted, except in rarest instances. The whole sentiment of early craft degenerated to a sentimentality having no longer decent significance nor commercial integrity; in fact all that is fussy, maudlin, and animal, basing its existence chiefly on vanity and ignorance.

Now let us learn from the machine. It teaches us that the beauty of wood lies first in its qualities as wood. No treatment that does not bring out these qualities all the time can be plastic or appropriate or beautiful. The machine teaches us that certain simple forms and handling are suitable to bring out the beauty of wood and certain forms are not; that all wood-carving is apt to be a forcing of the material, an insult to its finer possibilities as a material having in itself intrinsically artistic properties, of which its beautiful marking is one, its texture another, its color a third.

The machine, by its wonderful cutting, shaping, smoothing, and repetitive capacity, has made it possible so to use it without waste that the poor as well as the rich may enjoy to-day beautiful surface treatments of clean, strong forms that the branch veneers of Sheraton and Chippendale only hinted at, with dire extravagance, and which the middle ages utterly ignored. The machine has emancipated these beauties of nature in wood; made it possible to wipe out the mass of meaningless torture to which wood has been subjected since the world began, for it has been universally abused and maltreated by all peoples but the Japanese. Rightly appreciated, is not this the very process of elimination for which Morris pleaded?

And how fares the troop of old materials galvanized into new life by the machine? Our modern materials are these old materials in more plastic guise, rendered so by the machine, itself creating the very quality needed in material to satisfy its own art equation.

Who can sound the possibilities of burned clay, which the modern machine has rendered as sensitive to the creative brain as a dry plate to the lens—a marvelous simplifier? And this plastic covering material, cement, another simplifier, enabling the artist to clothe the structural frame with a simple, modestly beautiful robe where before he dragged in, as he does still drag in, five different kinds of material to compose one little cottage, pettily arranging it in an aggregation supposed to be picturesque—as a matter of fact, millinery, to be warped and beaten by sun, wind, and rain into a variegated heap of trash. Then there is the process of modern casting in metal—one of the perfected modern machines, capable of any form to which fluid will flow, to perpetuate the imagery of the most delicately poetic mind without let or hindrance—within reach of every one, therefore insulted and outraged by the bungler forcing it to a degraded seat at his degenerate festival.

Multitudes of processes are expectantly awaiting the sympathetic interpretation of the master mind; the galvano-plastic and its electrical brethren, a prolific horde, now cheap fakirs imitating real bronzes and all manner of the antique. Electro-glazing, a machine shunned because too cleanly and delicate for the clumsy hand of the traditional designer, who depends upon the mass and blur of leading to conceal his lack of touch. That delicate thing, the lithograph—the prince of a whole reproductive province of processes—see what this process becomes in the hands of a master like Whistler. He has sounded but one note in the gamut of its possibilities, but that product is intrinsically true to the process, and as delicate as the butterfly's wing.

So spins a rough, feeble thread of the evidence at large to the effect that the machine has weakened the artist; all but destroyed his hand-made art, if not its ideals, although he has made enough mischief meanwhile. These evident instances should serve to hint, at least to the thinking mind, that the machine is a marvelous simplifier; the emancipator of the creative mind, and in time the regenerator of the creative conscience.

Now, let us ask ourselves whether the fear of the higher artistic expression demanded by the machine, so thoroughly grounded in the arts and crafts, is founded upon a finely guarded reticence, a recognition of inherent weakness or plain ignorance? Let us, to be just, assume that it is equal parts of all three, and try to imagine an arts and crafts society that may educate itself to prepare to make some good impression upon the machine, the destroyer of their present ideals and tendencies, their salvation in disguise.

Such a society will, of course, be a society for mutual education. Exhibitions will not be a feature of its programme for years, for there will be nothing to exhibit except the shortcomings of the society, and they will hardly prove either instructive or amusing at this stage of proceedings. This society must, from the very nature of the proposition, be made up of the people who are in the work—that is, the manufacturers—coming into touch with such of those who assume the practice of the fine arts as profess a fair sense of the obligation to the public such assumption carries with it, and sociological workers whose interests are ever closely allied with art, as their prophets

Morris, Ruskin, and Tolstoy evince, and all those who have as personal graces and accomplishment perfected handicraft, whether fashion old or fashion new.

I suppose, first of all, the thing would resemble a debating society, or something even less dignified, until some one should suggest that it was time to quit talking and proceed to do something, which in this case would not mean giving an exhibition, but rather excursions to factories and a study of processes in place—that is, the machine in processes too numerous to mention, at the factories with the men who organize and direct them, but not in the spirit of the idea that these things are all gone wrong, looking for that in them which would most nearly approximate the handicraft ideal; not looking into them with even the thought of handicraft, and not particulary looking for craftsmen, but getting a scientific ground-plan of the process in mind, if possible, with a view to its natural bent and possibilities.

I will venture to say, from personal observation and some experience, that not one artist in one hundred has taken pains to thus educate himself. I will go further and say what I believe to be true, that not one educational institution in America has as yet attempted to forge the connecting link between science and art by training the artist to his actual tools, or, by a process of nature-study that develops in him the power of independent thought, fitting him to use them properly.

So let us call these preliminaries a process by which artists receive information nine-tenths of them lack concerning the tools they have to work with to-day—for tools to-day are processes and machines where they were once a hammer and a gouge. This proceeding doubtless would be of far more educational value to the artist than to the manufacturer, at least for some time to come, for there would be a difficult adjustment to make on the part of the artist and an attitude to change. So many artists are chiefly "attitude" that some would undoubtedly disappear with the attitude.

Granting that a determined, dauntless body of artist material could be brought together with sufficient persistent enthusiasm to grapple with the machine, would not some one be found who would provide the suitable experimental station (which is what the modern arts and crafts shop should be)—an experimental station that would represent in miniature the elements of this great pulsating web of the machine, where each pregnant process or significant tool in printing, lithography, galvano-electro processes, wood and steel working machinery, muffles and kilns would have its place, and where the best young scientific blood could mingle with the best and truest artistic inspiration, to sound the depths of these things, to accord them the patient, sympathetic treatment that is their due?

To me, the artist is he who can truthfully idealize the common sense of these tendencies in his chosen way. So I feel conception and composition to be simply the essence of refinement in organization, the original impulse of which may be registered by the artistic nature as unconsciously as the magnetic needle vibrates to the magnetic law, but which is, in synthesis or analysis, organically consistent, given the power to see it or not. And I have come to believe that the world of art, which we are so fond of calling the world outside of science, is not so much outside as it is the very heart quality of this great material growth—as religion is its conscience.

Look out over the modern city at nightfall from the top of a great down-town office building, and you may see at a glance how organic the machine has become, how interwoven it is in the warp and woof of our civilization, its essential tool indeed, if not the very framework of civilization itself.

Thus is the machine, the forerunner of democracy, into which the forces of art are to breathe the thrill of ideality—a soul.

FRANK LLOYD WRIGHT.

THE CIGARETTE GIRL
By Anders Zorn

THE NEW YORK ART WORLD—II

An artist's studio is often a place of charm and fascination. The flavor of bohemianism pervades it—to the mind of many. On the contrary, it is generally a place of serious work; an artist's life is not all "beer and skittles." True, the younger men believe in the old

IN THE SCOTCH HIGHLANDS
By G. Glenn Newell

adage that a little nonsense now and then is a tonic to the more serious brain faculties, and the "devil's Welsh," which Shakespeare thought to be humorous, is often spoken by them.

There is more. Let me take you to a well-known New York studio. There are the usual hangings of richly colored stuffs on the wall, oddly carved chairs, those exquisite knickknacks which caught an artist's fancy scattered about; the high light of the large window falls strongly in the middle of the room, where before his easel, propped up in a low chair, sits Robert C. Minor. Trouble has come to him of late in great measure. Bodily ailments have withered his frame, and sorrow crushed his heart when bereft of his life-companion some months ago. Still, sweetly sings this poet of the brush before the canvas, and the landscape depicted breathes the inspiration of delicate tenderness. How virile and strong he has been in his woodland stretches, how powerful in his skyscapes hovering over the tree copses, how brilliant in his handling of the sunset-glow bursting through dark verdure. On the canvas before which we are now sitting there is hovering the gray mist of a fading day, the placid water in the wood-

UPLAND FIELDS
By Alexander Schilling

land pool is gently rippled by the puffing breeze, maybe the tall beeches somewhat droop their branches after the heat of afternoon; yet all is so restful, quiet, and lovable. Thus the artist paints his own soul.

His reward has come with the years. It is not so many years ago when Minor was rejected by the high and mighty juries of academy and society. His erstwhile judges we may not know, but his work has outstripped theirs, and is now sought for, surpassing the limit of his productive power. And his physical frailness is surrounded with the comforts of prosperity.

WHEN DAY IS DONE
By W. H. Drake

BAVENO, LAKE MAGGIORE
George H. Smillie

Another studio? Here we are at St. John's. The apostolic name is prefixed by J. Allen. He is a long, laughing, merry-andrew, busying about through the bluish haze made heavy by the cigarette smoke and the burning Japanese incense sticks, attending the punch-bowl and the comforts of his guests. A. H. Maurer, with Mephistophelean countenance suffused by an angelic smile, recounts the latest yarns of the Bal Bullier and of the Parisian *Quartier*, whence he returned but a few months ago; F. Luis Mora walks the human hair as Signor Agostino used to do it in the circus; G. Glenn Newell throws in some dry jokes that make us shake; Hy. Mayer, the caricaturist, tells his telephone story and gives absolutely perfect imitations of famous people, from the late Queen Victoria to Oom Paul Kruger and George Inness, Jr., the president of the Salmagundi Club; and over there sits Albert L. Groll, quiet and happy. The brushes are laid aside, and these men "in the foreground of human life," laugh care to scorn, and in the buoyancy of their hopes turn like marigolds toward the sunny side. How bright life gleams with its illusions, aspirations, dreams!

Yet these faces at other times wear the stern expression of determination and strength. They have all shown their mettle, some plucked laurels in the struggle. Against the wall stands St. John's "Alice in Wonderland." A young girl of about ten years is depicted sitting in a high-backed chair, her hands resting on the arms of the chair. In her eyes is the far-away look which sees the fairy visions of which she has just read in the story-books scattered on the floor at her feet. The whole is in a quiet color scheme and of a serious impression. There is excellent drawing; the background is unobtrusive.

Then there is Maurer. A young man filled with serious ideals, he seeks expression in a tonal quality of work which is convincing. When first he went to Paris he entered Julian's, but found after a week or so that no good but much harm would come to him, and he let the schools alone and studied the masters at the Louvre. The result—a wonderful power over his pigment, which he controls with dexterity. When he came home this winter and saw the trend of art here accepted by the miscellaneous buyer, he felt like giving up. "There is no hope for me," he plaintively laments. But he sends a canvas to the Salmagundi Club exhibition, where out of a hundred and more pictures it receives the Inness, Jr., prize; he sends three canvases to the Society of American Artists' exhibition, and while nine hundred out of thirteen hundred canvases are rejected, all three are marked "one" by the jury, and,—credit to the hanging committee—all three are hung on the line.

This is not luck! It is the recognition of sterling worth. There is scarcely a man with such power over values, such looseness, such freedom of handling. His work makes one think of Whistler's portrait of his mother, yet so vastly differing in its method that the likeness is only suggested, and not to be found in imitation of the pyrotechnic master. The future has to reckon with this young man.

I spoke last month of F. Luis Mora's work. The mural painting which adorns the public library in Lynn, Massachusetts, shows the ambitious manner in which this artist carries out his inventions. It represents "The Awakening of Ignorance," and is a well-thought-out

ROCKY MOUNTAIN SHEEP
By A. Phimister Proctor

scheme of excellent draughtsmanship. Hy. Mayer has brought along an advance copy of a children's book, now published by E. P. Dutton. It is entitled "A Trip to Toyland," and relates a healthy dream of a youngster anent his toys. The graceful lines of Mayer's pen are in evidence in the illustrations, and must convey even to the baby-mind the first principles of beauty in the artist's flowing and sweeping curves.

Albert L. Groll has not quite arrived. His work varies in treatment, although some of it is important, as it has hung on the line at the Academy. A recent exhibit of twenty-one of his sketches at the

Chicago Art Institute attracted considerable attention from the local critics, especially his "Old Road to Schleisheim," which is loose in

"THEN ARISE—THE LARK IS SHAKING SUNLIT WINGS"
By A. M. Turner

handling, of excellent color and pleasing design. His work deserves praise for its outdoor feeling, its sincere portrayal of nature, the charm

SUNSET NEAR MORET, FRANCE
By George H. McCord

PASSING THE OUTPOSTS
By E. L. Henry

which invests a brush without mannerism. To the observant eye of the critical collector there is the earnest of great merit, and even the inquiring amateur compares the honesty of purpose and poetic simplicity of his outdoor work with belabored reproductions of studio compositions.

G. Glenn Newell is a painter of the bovine race. I had just that morning seen at his studio the lay-in of a large cattle picture—some cows in a meadow. Originally he painted still-life, but the longer one seeks to escape from one's *métier*, the surer the grasp when the natural bent has free course. So he has come to interpret faultlessly the philosophical indolence, the calm resignation, the vagueness of look of the patient milk-givers, or the fiery eye, the heavy, cumbrous tread of a storm-stampeded herd in the Scottish Highlands. Not a clear day passes that he is not out on the Jersey meadows studying his favorite models. And then we all join in the chorus: "For he's a jolly good fellow!"

The best time to visit an artist in his studio for a quiet chat, while not keeping him from his work, is on a dark, rainy day. With pipes lit and something between us, we loll back in the easy-chairs in *dolce far niente*. All around hang kimonos, tapestries, odd weapons; the model-throne is pushed in the corner, my hat hangs on the left ear of the life-size lay-figure, rugs cover the floor, screens are about, the whole studio becomes a cozy corner.

He is a great talker, my vis-à-vis, who shall remain nameless, when he lets loose, and an excellent worker for all that. Something has disgruntled him, and as we are settled—

"What do you think of that close corporation affair up in Buffalo? Call that a representative American art exhibition? It is nothing of the kind. Just thirty-eight pictures out of the many hundreds submitted to the jury have been accepted. The whole show is made up of pictures invited from friends and acquaintances of the management. I know of pictures, accepted by a half-dozen juries in as many principal cities, that were turned down and crowded out at Buffalo. It is just like it is in Paris. All you need is a pull. Go to one of the masters—coddle him and you get into the Salon; coddle some more and you get a mention. What is the use trying to paint when eternal jealousy and politics will shut the door in your face."

But honest Jack is only in a funk. He'll beat the combination yet and get out on top.

We have been fortunate of late in the exhibitions, which give a fair résumé of what the men are doing. There is decided progress all along the line. Paris last year was an eye-opener to the Continent as far as knowledge of the American school went, and the Academy and Society of American Artists shows, as well as the exhibitions of the Water Color Society, of the Salmagundi Club, of "The Ten," and of the "Landscape Painters," hold well up to like exhibitions

THE GOLDEN BAR OF EVENING
By F. K. M. Rehn

THE FOLD
By Frank Russell Green

abroad. The Society exhibition is not so numerous but of more sustained value than last year's Royal Academy in London.

It is noteworthy that our men are looking more and more for tone in their work. Examples of this at the Society were a portrait by H. M. Walcott, a magnificent "Autumn Twilight" by Henry Golden Dearth, Jules Wengel's "Evening on the Canche," a landscape with running water in Thaulow's style. Addison T. Millar, just returned from abroad, has astounded his *confrères* by the vast strides he has made, as signalized in his "Moonrise, Blaricum." E. Irving Couse glazes, yet is sincere. W. Merritt Post shows also his feeling for quality in "Slow Declining Day," and John Noble Barlow, while following too much the English method in his "Dorset Meadows," is wholly convincing and satisfactory in his "Cornish Lane."

Another young artist, but a rising painter withal, to be singled out, is John G. Saxton, who exhibited "The Return Home" and "The Watering Place," the latter being a luminous bit with correctly drawn figures and a thin, light atmosphere. Likewise Robert Henri has two canvases which bespeak great talent, with a Manet influence. Really the best landscape in this exhibition was Ben Foster's "Mists of the Morning."

At the Water Color Society, the work of Frank Russell Green, F. K. M. Rehn, Will Robinson, Harry Fenn, George McCord. Edward Moran, E. H. Pothast, and others made this one of the best aggregations of sheets in the lighter medium ever brought together.

Conversing last summer with a foreign artist upon the subject of topographical painting in America, he observed that the picturesqueness of the ancient towns of the Continent, so attractive to American artists, should convince them that the equally picturesque views of American scenery and American cities would be avidiously demanded by continental buyers. He pointed to Homer Lee's "Building of a Skyscraper," Schreyvogel's "My Bunkie," and some other canvases in the American section in Paris, which attracted great attention, as cases in point. Would there had been some of Thomas Moran's Yellowstone scenery to speak of the grandeur of our great West!

DAVID C. PREYER.

CLEVER WORK OF STUDENTS

Much clever work is done by students at the various schools that never gets to the general public, since it is designed for issuance in catalogues or annuals which have a special or limited circulation. These drawings are worthy of presentation to a wider circle of art lovers than that which would see them in the natural course of events. The following are published by permission from a forthcoming yearbook, and are suggestive of what the student classes are doing:

FRESHMEN

THE COLLEGE YEARS—1
Drawn for "The Integral," Published by Armour Institute of Technology
By W. C. Barbour, Student at School of Illustration, Chicago

THE COLLEGE YEARS—II
Drawn for "The Integral," Published by Armour Institute of Technology
By W. C. Harbour, Student at School of Illustration, Chicago

THE COLLEGE YEARS—III
Drawn for "The Integral," Published by Armour Institute of Technology
By W. C. Barbour, Student at School of Illustration, Chicago

THE COLLEGE YEARS—IV
Drawn for "The Integral," Published by Armour Institute of Technology
By W. C. Barbour, Student at School of Illustration, Chicago

ALEXANDER POPE, PAINTER OF ANIMALS

No American artist has attained higher distinction as a painter of animals than Alexander Pope. A born sportsman and a lover of brute creation, his art is a direct outgrowth of his affection for the animals he delights to limn. He is not a graduate of the art schools; but self-taught, with the exception of two quarters of instruction in perspective drawing and one quarter with Dr. Rimmer in anatomy, he passed from mercantile life to the studio.

Many of the favored of salons and exhibitions would perhaps deny to him a high rank as a painter, but if the skillful portraitists of humankind merit the mead of laudation bestowed upon them, certainly Pope is worthy of the highest praise for his animal portraits; if the works of a Landseer and a Bonheur give them justly the rank commonly assigned to them as creative artists, many of Pope's more pretentious pictures entitle him to a higher place in the roll of honor than critics have usually conceded to him.

STUDIO OF ALEXANDER POPE

Pope's paintings are not of the conventional chromo type one is wont to note in animal pictures. They are careful studies, absolutely faithful to his subjects, full of life, spirit, character. The reason is not far to seek. He is a master of animal anatomy and is a good draughtsman, and his lively imagination lends dramatic force to his compositions. Animals evince as sharply defined individual traits as human beings, give just as much evidence of character; and of these traits Pope has been an enthusiastic student. As a consequence, through long practice, he has developed the faculty of investing his animal pictures with much of the charm of character studies.

What is equally noteworthy, Pope has been no seeker after ephemeral notoriety, but has ever been an honest, serious worker on

MARTYRDOM OF ST. EUPHEMIA
By Alexander Pope

legitimate lines. The commissions intrusted to him have not been heralded by press notices, nor, with occasional exceptions, has the fame of his finished works been bruited abroad. He has simply been content patiently to study and work in his Boston studio and to find more glory in self-satisfaction than in notoriety. He has, it is true, painted many of what he calls "characteristic pieces," in which skillful imitation has been more pronounced than creative effort, but primarily he has aimed to be an interpreter and portrayer of animal life, and he has succeeded.

Passing as he did direct from a mercantile to a professional calling without the intervention of the usual years of artistic training, it is not to be supposed that Pope suddenly discovered a natural gift and was genius enough to dispense with the ordinary courses of instruction. He did not awake to find himself famous, nor did he suddenly discover in the routine of his business pursuits that he had exceptional talent for drawing and color-work. His art has been a slow development, and he has worked hard for all that he has attained.

He was born in Boston in 1849, and as a child of seven years of age did creditable work in sketching animals. He showed even in these early efforts a fair grasp of the principles of his art. The uncertainties of professional life, however, were such as to lead his parents to discourage any ambition the boy may have had to follow art as anything but a pleasant avocation, and his entering the lumber business with his father shortly after graduating from the high school was the result. Several years of uncongenial work followed, and these sufficed to teach young Pope that business was not his forte and to convince him that for him an artist's career was not more hazardous than the pursuits in which he was engaged.

His early years of effort were naturally marked with more or less experimenting. At twenty he was a devotee of wood-carving and modeling, coloring his finished works true to nature. His love of outdoor life and sports naturally led him for a time to select domestic animals and game for his models. His success was marked almost from the outset, and many of his pieces of carving and modeling found abiding resting-places in important collections, one or more of his works, it is interesting to note, finding their way to the dining-hall of the Czar of Russia. The accuracy of his modeling, the delicacy of his touch, the masterful way in which he manipulated his material so as to incorporate in his works those individual animal traits that have since more fully characterized his paintings, gave him a certain vogue with lovers of this form of sculpture and misled him for a time into attempts in which he was less successful.

He was seized with an ambition to become a sculptor of the human form, and made many a study of a fair degree of excellence. Indeed, in 1881 and 1882 he successfully executed a number of busts, but in these undertakings he failed to realize his own ideal, and his work soon drifted into the specialty with which his name has since been connected. One of the illustrations accompanying this article, the Kensington lions, executed for Henry Bigelow Williams, of Boston, give evidence of no mean ability in sculpture. But this form of artistic expression was ultimately all but abandoned for what to the artist was the more congenial and fascinating work of depicting his pets in color.

Up to 1886 the artist's efforts with the palette were limited to the painting of dogs and birds by special commission. In the fall of this year, however, Pope produced his first notable canvas, "Calling Out the Hounds," which was widely exhibited, and which excited the most favorable comment, not merely by its composition and coloring, but by its life and spirit. The artist had arrived at that point in his career when he felt impelled to do something more pretentious than painting somebody's animal on order, and he prepared for the execution of this canvas in the most thorough way possible. He made a careful study of costumes, the manners of the hunt, the action of dogs—everything needful to make an accurate and spirited picture. The painting was bright with color, vigorous, decorative, and it soon was accorded a place in the Boston Tavern, where it was generally admired.

KENSINGTON LIONS
By Alexander Pope

The success of this first venture in the line of creative work impelled Pope to break away more and more from the narrow field of an animal portraitist. He continued, of course, to take commissions for animal portraits, but he at the same time kept persistently at work broadening his scope and essaying to paint pictures full of life and incident. It was while making these attempts, apparently, that the artist discovered his wonderful facility in depicting texture and in producing illusions, with the result that he rapidly turned out a number of exhibition pictures of still life which gained him the

SETTER RETRIEVING A PHEASANT
By Alexander Pope

plaudits of the public, but which were a witness rather of his cleverness with the brush than of his ability as an artist in the best sense.

Pope's ambition to become a painter of pictures had its influence on his animal portraits. He sought, and for the most part succeeded in an admirable degree, to put his subjects in a picturesque setting in keeping with the character of the animals portrayed, and calculated to take off the baldness of mere portraits. Many of his pictures, therefore, of dogs, birds, and horses, painted to appease the vanity or satisfy the love of his patrons for their favorites, have thus a dis-

WAITING FOR ORDERS
By Alexander Pope

tinct value as works of art. Combined with fine draughtsmanship and fidelity of coloring are charming bits of landscape, peeps into copses, banks of sedge, sunlit sheets of water, and the like, which suggest an ideal composition rather than a prosaic likeness.

Detailed reference to the artist's many canvases cannot here be made, but the essential qualities of a few pictures will give a suggestion of the many. His "Just from Town" may be cited as one of his simpler and withal most pleasing paintings. It depicts simply two peacocks with their gorgeous plumage showing brilliantly against a daisy-dashed meadow. The birds of fine feathers are supposed by courtesy of imagination to typify the city folk who sometimes visit their country cousins and assume the airs of superiority. In this case the only visible country cousins are a couple of rabbits, half lost in the weeds and foliage, which seem surprised and somewhat abashed at the brilliant dress of the visitors in comparison with their own tawny skins. A pleasing landscape leads off into the distance, and an equally pleasing foreground of grass and flowers complete the striking composition. It is simply a pictorial depiction of a human trait in terms of animal life.

"The Truant" is another canvas, essentially different, but having a similar underlying conception. It represents two English setters, one of which, a truant to the chase, and betraying the fact in his every look, stands in a pool of water, sharply outlined against a background of bank and alder-bushes. Through the underbrush the other dog emerges, with manifest surprise at discovering his mate paddling in the water instead of attending to his proper business. The abashed, guilty look of the culprit and the alert, reproving face of the discoverer are admirably depicted. Here again the composition is studied for effect, but eminently natural and effective.

Doubtless Pope's two most notable pictures are his "Martyrdom of St. Euphemia" and his "Glaucus and the Lion." Both are dramatic incidents forcefully depicted, which appeal to the spectator not less from the masterful execution of the artist than from the worth of the conception embodied. Of the "Martyrdom" the accompanying illustration gives a suggestion. It is Pope's favorite among his many works. His "Glaucus," a theme taken from Bulwer's "Last Days of Pompeii," is an attempt to depict a moment of irresolution, if not of fear, on the part of a lion in the arena. Glaucus, nude but for a cincture about the loins, stands, dagger in hand, on the sand, with the serried spectators behind him as a background. The lion occupies the immediate foreground, manifestly intimidated and betraying his fear in his trembling attitude and faltering half-averted glance. The situation is dramatic in the extreme, and is pictorially told with all the force that a strong historical imagination, coupled with a sureness of the means of narration employed, could impart to the canvas.

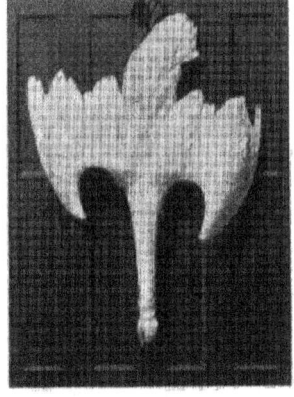

A WHITE SWAN
By Alexander Pope

IN LEASH
By Alexander Pope

In these more elaborate paintings, as in his minor works, the artist's knowledge of animal anatomy and characteristics is quite exceptional. This mastery of animal life, artistically speaking, is the evidence of untiring effort. Having once determined on a specialty, Pope devoted his every energy toward acquiring that knowledge which would qualify him to paint his subjects to the life.

America has produced no better teacher of artistic anatomy than Dr. Rimmer, and Pope was an apt pupil. The fundamental grounding he received from his teacher he supplemented by individual study and constant practice. He haunted the stables, the aviaries, and the kennels, and day after day made studies of his subjects in every conceivable posture. He spent weeks in the zoölogical gardens of New York and Philadelphia, and also at Barnum's winter headquarters at Bridgeport, Connecticut, painting wild animals, and especially lions.

In undertaking to transfer his conceptions to canvas, therefore, he is in position to rely upon his own intimate knowledge; and be it said to his credit, he has never essayed to paint subjects for the details of which he would have to become a copyist.

Of Pope's "characteristic pieces" little need here be said. They are certainly marvelous in the illusions they produce. They are, however (and the artist frankly admits it), tricks of the palette rather than strong conceptions ably expressed. One of Pope's favorite pastimes is to paint firearms, birds, rabbits, and the like hanging to a slate-colored door, and cause them to stand out with a semblance to reality that deceives the sense of sight. In these feats the effect is produced partly by a skillful manipulation of shadows and partly by a faithfulness in the matter of texture that comes from careful study.

One of his last, as it is one of his most realistic, productions of this class, is the painting of a white swan hanging to a door. There is nothing to lend attractiveness to the picture save the beauty of outline and the delicacy of the white plumage. No background could be more commonplace or uninteresting. The texture of the plumage, however, is perfect, and the outline of the bird in its simplicity is faultless. There are no telltale witnesses of deception, yet at close range the average spectator would cheat himself into believing that a real bird hung before him.

It is not works of this sort, however, in which Pope prides himself. Primarily he wishes to be a faithful interpreter of animal life, and in this field, which is certainly worthy of the highest art, he has few equals.

Howard J. Cave.

WORK OF THE YOUNGER ARCHITECTS

The fourteenth annual exhibition recently held by the Chicago Architectural Club at the Art Institute compared favorably with its predecessors, and marked an improvement over them in several respects. One of these was the reduction in wall-space covered, chiefly by the omission of the usual quota of great projects from the various architectural schools, which to the average visitor have a

PANEL FROM A DECORATION FOR A BILLIARD-ROOM
IN ROCHESTER, N. Y.
By Harvey Ellis

rather monotonous sameness in design and in manner of presentation. Another was the grouping of the more pictorial drawings and sketches of the local men in a small room by themselves.

The "Book of the Exhibition" has again changed its form, and between very elegant and tasteful board covers text and plates are beautifully printed, as they were last year, without a line of advertising matter to mar their effect. For this result, successfully achieved a second time by the club, and as yet by no other architectural club in the country, the numerous patrons who subscribed to the exhibition fund deserve hearty thanks. The book also bears evidence of careful editing, the work being done this year chiefly by Hugh Garden.

SCHEME FOR DECORATION
By Frank L. Linden

For text, as a foil to the illustrations, is published, with illuminated initials, Frank Wright's paper on "The Art and Craft of the Machine," an abridgment of which is reprinted in this issue of BRUSH AND PENCIL. From the illustrations, some sixty in number, the accompanying pictures have been taken, for their architectural or pictorial interest, or both.

From a pictorial standpoint, the collection of drawings contributed by Willis Polk, of San Francisco, attracted more attention on the part of the architects of Chicago than anything from the hands of their colleagues. For boldness, freedom, and beauty of technique, without hard contrast or forced effects, they have not been surpassed by any American architect. Most noteworthy are the great drawing of the peristyle for the San Francisco market-place and the rough study for a Catholic church. A series of five studies for a bank building by the same architect shows a most commendable zeal in endeavoring to solve an impossible problem—the setting of a Roman temple portico in the middle of a row of hodge-podge American mercantile buildings of the cast-iron Renaissance and Victorian Gothic periods. They have just tried the same thing in Chicago, and some very good people doubtless insist that the thing, having actually been done, is certainly possible. But one may trust that they will in time discover their error. It is not to be hoped that the Roman temple will be made harmonious with its fellow-buildings by a wave of classic renewal which shall give the "followers of Phidias" full sway over entire mercantile blocks in business districts.

This war of the styles, this clash of the schools, and of no schools, brings forward naturally for consideration the work of the Chicago Architectural Club, past, present, and prospective, and its actual as well as

HOUSE AT LAKE FOREST, ILL.
John T. Hetherington, Architect

HOUSE AT LA SALLE, ILL.
Pond & Pond, Architects

WORK OF THE YOUNGER ARCHITECTS

its possible influence as a factor in the development of a local, possibly of a national, architecture.

Originally merely a draughtsman's sketch club, this organization has thriven and kept pace with the progress of the similar clubs in Boston, New York, and Philadelphia, profiting by their example and by their experiments, and making innovations of its own in turn, which have set a pace for the eastern men. Under the presidency of George R. Dean, the club first began to broaden its field of action, and under his enthusiastic leadership of a "squad" of constant draughtsmen, the club's admirable plan for the improvement of the Chicago lake front was completed, as delineated in the splendid bird's-eye water-color by Hugh Garden. Soon after the club acquired its very comfortable and advantageous quarters in the Art Institute, and with its various classes and competitions has done each year much valuable and earnest work.

While the older architects, with their established reputation and large commissions have been putting up big buildings, these younger architects and draughtsmen, still little known to the public, have been developing their knowledge and skill, cultivating their finer perceptions of

A HOUSE AT HIGHLAND PARK, ILL.
Hugh M. G. Garden, Architect

beauty, and trying to solve seriously some of the problems of modern municipal architecture which in the rush of commercialism are permitted to go by default.

In the winter of 1898, eight or ten of the older men, all practicing architects, arranged to take in hand certain problems in design, each choosing by lot six or eight of the younger members to assist him, each group being designated as a "squad," and each leader as a "patron." A number of interesting projects were successfully worked out, each patron being given an evening at the club for showing the work of his "squad" and explaining it in detail, a general discussion following. Among the problems of public interest thoughtfully handled were a great central produce market and warehouse for rail, boat, and city traffic, under Dwight H. Perkins; an elevated loop railway station for State and Van Buren streets, under Robert C. Spencer, Jr.; and an extension of the Art Institute, under Edward M. Garden.

Last year's annual exhibition was probably the most interesting ever held by the club, augmented as it was by the splendid collection of photographic drawings and models of old and new tenements and cottages by the Improved Housing Association, and the Arts and Crafts Society's furnished tenement. For the first time was exhibited also the remarkably beautiful and unique pottery produced experimentally by Mr. Gates and his associates of the American Terra-Cotta and Ceramic Company, at their kilns near Crystal Lake, Illinois. The old club catalogue, with its border of advertising matter marring many pages, gave place to the first "Book of the Exhibition," published entirely through the generosity of patrons interested in promoting public interest in good architecture. To the array of illustrations were added several special articles on topics of interest to architects, making the book a valuable souvenir of a noteworthy exhibition, the most unique and interesting individual architectural feature of which was the work of Frank Lloyd Wright.

Closely following this exhibition came the first annual convention of the year-old Architectural League of America, a federation of architectural clubs, formed in 1899 at Cleveland. The work of the convention perfected the organization and was attended with marked enthusiasm, the Chicago club taking a prominent part in the proceedings, and contributing a strong impulse in the direction of the so-called "new movement" in architecture as distinguished from the widespread fashion-mongering of the commercially successful "great architects" of to-day. Mr. Wright's paper, read before the convention, and Mr. Sullivan's address at the Auditorium banquet, certainly appeared to add fresh strength to the growing revolt against the present universal blind following of dry precedent in modern building, regardless of the development of new materials, new methods of construction, and new needs.

In the selection of the League's governing body for the year now ending Chicago was equally honored, Joseph C. Llewellyn being chosen president of the League. With him have served upon the executive committee of the League, Hugh M. G. Garden, Richard G. Schmidt, Emil Lorsch, and Robert C. Spencer, Jr. Mr. Llewellyn and Mr. Spencer will represent Chicago at the coming convention of the League to be held at Philadelphia in May, where the work of the committee on education will doubtless bring forth many suggestions helpful to the schools and to the profession, through the various addresses being prepared for the occasion on the special topics assigned to the various clubs for discussion and through the debates likely to follow the reading of these addresses.

To New York, Philadelphia, and Chicago were assigned the questions, "Should the study of architectural design and of the historic styles follow and be based upon a knowledge of pure design?" and "How can pure design best be studied?" An interesting evening was spent at the club not long ago in discussing these questions, which are awakening a powerful interest among the younger men in the profession, and through Mr. Spencer as her representative at Philadelphia, Chicago will advocate the affirmative, as opposed to the present methods of the leading architectural schools here and abroad.

From the foregoing rough outline of its work during recent years, it will be seen by those who have paid a little attention to such matters that in the Architectural Club Chicago has a large and enthusiastic body of workers in a very trying and uncertain field, an organization thoroughly alive, energetic, and ready to do much to abolish civic ugliness and add to civic beauty, if given the chance. In proof of this the gratuitous designing of shelter and playground inclosures for the small parks commission by members of the club and the work done on other municipal problems bear strong witness.

Yet the architect members of the club fail to receive from the public any substantial recognition of the artistic merits of their work as exemplified in their contributions to the annual exhibitions at the Art Institute. In architectural as in pictorial and plastic art, Chicagoans do not yet seem to show much appreciation of mere talent unattended by social or commercial prestige, and only seeks those who have in some way acquired fame, whether deserved or not. In fact, the architects sympathize keenly with the artists in their cry for a more intelligent and discriminating public, a public interested in architecture as a fine art rather than as mere building for investment or commercial purposes.

In these annual exhibitions the local contributors have learned that no commissions will come to them through such a showing of their work. And yet in any great city, where a young architect's buildings are few and widely scattered, he can only become known to an interested and discriminating public by some such exhibition of drawings and photographs of his work. Very few ever see his buildings until he "arrives," builds downtown, and has a great vogue, and becomes too successful and too commercial to study his work or to stamp it with his own genius and individuality.

May the day come when the rising architectural genius may receive commissions from appreciative strangers on the strength and beauty of his work as shown on paper at these public exhibitions which are free to all citizens. Our cities would gain beauty through early recognition and substantial encouragement of talent on the part of their citizens, and successful mediocrity would receive less beyond its due reward.

ROBERT C. SPENCER, JR.

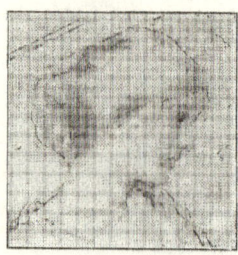

FRAGMENT FROM A DECORATION
By Harvey Ellis

CATHEDRAL OF DORDRECHT
By Charles Storm van Gravesande

GALLERY OF ETCHINGS
Plate Fifteen

Brush and Pencil

EVOLUTION OF A PICTURE — A CHAPTER ON STUDIES

Many people who consider themselves well informed upon matters of art have but the vaguest conceptions of the way in which a picture is made. An artist does not sit down with palette, brushes, and canvas and dash off a picture when an inspiration seizes him. A sketch may be made in this way for the mere pleasure of doing it, or in order that the data which are thus secured may be preserved for future use, but the process of making a picture is longer and much more elaborate.

The picture which expresses something, which has a *raison d'etre*, is generally evolved with as much thought and care as a writer bestows on a serious article or a story and by somewhat similar processes. In a picture, whatever its subject may be, the "unities" are imposed by the means of expression. A picture cannot well represent more than one idea, one place, or one instant of time. All that the artist has to say must be concentrated into one single effect, and consequently all of his study must be in the direction of elimination from the multiplicity of suggestions which nature makes to him, the material for a picture.

STUDY
By Wilhelm Leibl

As some writers are able to complete the composition of their articles in their minds before they begin to put their thoughts on paper, there are artists who are able to see their pictures finished before they begin to paint, but they are rare exceptions.

STUDIES OF DRAPERY
By Frank X. Leyendecker

For any important pictures requiring arrangement or composition, as is the case of nearly all figure subjects, most artists make numerous studies. The title "Study" applied to paintings shown in exhibitions is nearly always a misnomer. Such works are chiefly the work of students or painters who have more technique than ideas to paint, and were not painted as a study for some thing more important.

When an artist has received his "inspiration," or found a motive and given the subject sufficient thought to have decided something of how it is to be treated, he generally makes a composition sketch, possibly several of them, before the arrangement of the picture is decided upon. These are almost always made "out of his head," without models, with only the memory of effects previously observed in nature to guide him.

From this point in the production of the picture there are various ways by which the artist may arrive at the completion of his work. He may either arrange his models in relation to the accessories as nearly as possible like his composition and paint directly from them, or he may "square up" or in some other manner transfer the lines of his composition to his canvas and proceed by painting portions of his picture directly from nature or from studies.

Making important changes in a picture after it is once commenced is not productive of so good results as a rapid execution preceded by mature preparation. It is for this reason that most artists who paint figure subjects make careful drawings of the various figures of their compositions, and many fragmentary studies of heads, hands, or other portions in which the expression of a pose or movement may play an

NUDE STUDY
By Edgar Cameron

important part in the picture. Studies of drapery, of accessories, of architecture or landscape which may constitute the setting for the figures, are other important elements in the preparation of a picture.

PORTRAIT STUDY
By F. A. von Kaulbach

When animals are introduced into a picture many studies of them are necessary because of the great difficulty in securing a suitable pose or action, owing to their almost constant movement.

Facial expression also requires much study. There are models who have sufficient of an actor's ability to enter into the spirit of an artist's conception and give him a pose or an expression which may be literally copied, but they are rare; and in order to secure exactly what he desires in this respect the artist often becomes his own model, with the aid of a mirror. The studies of facial expression shown here are parts of a series thus made by a young artist of Paris, who possessed considerable histrionic ability. They were published by him as a guide to artists and students.

It has been frequently remarked that the technical qualities of the painting of some students is superior to that of many artists who are

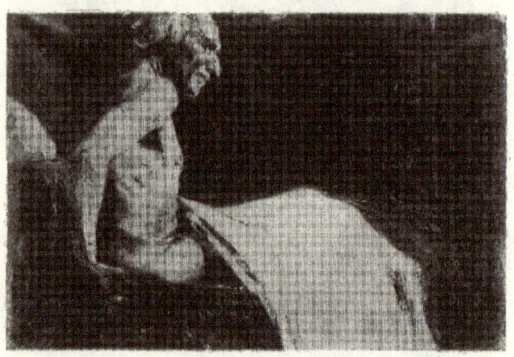

STUDY FOR A SICK MAN
By Jean Paul Laurens

accounted great masters, and yet their pictures are practically valueless except as examples of technique. The reason of this is that they have not learned to use their knowledge, and what is learned in an art school is but a small part of what an artist has to learn. Some masters, of whom Puvis de Chevannes is a striking example, have learned so well how to express their ideas that they dispense with technical elegance in their painting. Of Puvis de Chevannes it is sometimes wrongly held by immature critics that he was an incapable draughtsman.

Many artists, in order that the figures in their pictures may express more fully the sentiment of a pose, begin by making a careful drawing of the nude over which drapery or costume is afterward drawn from the draped or clothed model. There is preserved in the Louvre a

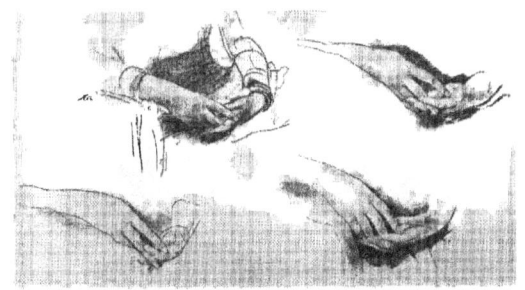

STUDIES OF HANDS
By F. A. von Kaulbach

STUDIES IN DRAPERY
By Sir Frederick Leighton

large unfinished picture by David, "Le Serment du jeu de Panme," in which all of the figures are carefully drawn in the nude and only the portrait heads are painted. It excites the risibility of most visitors to the gallery, but it is of interest to artist and students. Meissonier was so scrupulous in his drawing that he often modeled his

PORTRAIT STUDY
By Kasper Ritter

horses and sometimes his figures in wax from which to make his drawings.

In a subject in which there are numerous figures, animals, or objects of similar size, the element of correct perspective is of great importance, and the grouping together of maquettes, or small models in wax or clay, makes it possible to avoid those errors which creep into the work of some of the greatest artists. Sir Frederick Leighton frequently made use of the plan, and it is said that Detaille, in composing his battle scenes, arranges whole companies of pewter soldiers on a table on which the inequalities of the surface of the ground have been represented in various ways.

Maquettes and manikins are of great service in composing decorative subjects when it is desired to show figures in unusual positions requiring violent foreshortening, as in flying, or in a perspective system such as is sometimes used in ceiling decoration, with a vanishing paint in the air.

For the study of drapery they are also invaluable. An effect of flying movement may be given to drapery by laying it upon the floor and drawing it from above or by arranging it in suspension with strings, but a more effective model may be made of paper, which is sufficiently stiff to retain its folds long enough, without support, to permit it to be drawn. Its folds are sharper than those of cloth, but it has the advantage of

CHARACTER HEAD
By Leonardo da Vinci

STUDIES OF HEADS
By Fritz Roeber

more natural effects, and it is possible to find in tissue paper colors approaching almost any shade desired in a painting, or to tint or decorate it as one may wish with water-color.

Portrait painters frequently use large lay figures, upon which they place the costumes of their sitters, rarely for the purpose of making studies, but to serve as a substitute for the sitter in painting directly on the portrait. Other artists make use of the lay figure to make studies of elaborate costumes or uniforms.

In making studies of animal motion, many painters resort to the use of instantaneous photographs, with the result that they fre-

STUDIES OF TYPES
By J. F. Raffaelli

quently show movements too rapid to be observed by the human eye. In their efforts to avoid such solecisms, artists have resorted to various devices to study the motion of the animals they paint. Aimé Morot, who has painted some of the most spirited cavalry charges ever reproduced on canvas, was attached to the General Staff of the French army, and had all the horses and men he desired at his disposition. His favorite mode of study was to have horses ridden past him, and at a certain point he would give one quick glance at his models, close his eyes, and open them only when he had diverted his gaze to the white surface of the paper held in his lap on which he quickly jotted down the impression received. Meissonier had a track built, along which he had himself propelled as horses were ridden along a parallel course. Another excellent way for an artist to gain an appreciation of a horse's movement is to see and *feel* it at the same time by riding the animal along a wall in sunlight and observing its shadow.

It may be said that an artist never finds a model which corresponds exactly to his ideal, and he is obliged to make changes of form and expression in making his studies. Certain characteristics may be accentuated and others suppressed, while others which the model may not possess are supplied from memory, imagination, or from other models.

The ways of using studies when they are made are as various as the ways of making them. If a study is in the form of a drawing it may be copied directly in the picture, or it may be transferred either in its actual size by tracing or pouncing, or on a larger scale by "squaring up." In

Mirth

Contempt

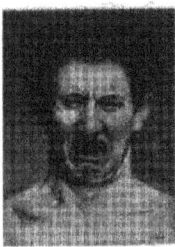

Disgust

STUDIES OF FACIAL EXPRESSION
By M. Hayman

STUDIES OF TYPES
By J. F. Raffaelli

squaring up, lines are drawn over the drawing to form squares and corresponding squares of a different proportion are drawn on the canvas where the picture is to be made. All of these processes admit of a certain amount of refinement, correction, or simplification of the original study, and anything which gives an artist an opportunity to prolong his preparations and shorten the time of the actual painting of a picture is of great benefit, as the result will be more spontaneous, fresher, and more vigorous than if it is puttered over and shows traces of experiment.

The artist's studies are the ammunition with which he loads up for a final effective *coup*, which makes a hit or a miss, as his aim has been true or not.

That such studies are requisite for good work is the universal verdict of all who have essayed to teach the art of painting. "It is undoubtedly a splendid and desirable accomplishment to be able to design instantaneously any given subject," says Sir Joshua Reynolds in his Twelfth Discourse. "It is an excellence that I believe every artist would wish to possess; but unluckily, the manner in which this dexterity is acquired habituates the mind to be contented with first thoughts, without choice or selection. The judgment, after it has been long passive, by degrees loses its power of becoming active when exertion is necessary. Whoever, therefore, has this talent must in some measure undo what he had the habit of doing, or at least give a new turn to his mind. Great works which are to live and stand the criticism of posterity are not performed at a heat. A proportionable time is required for deliberation and circumspection. . . . . However

EVOLUTION OF A PICTURE

extraordinary it may appear, it is certainly true that the inventions of the *pittori improvisatori*, as they may be called, have—notwithstanding the common boast of their authors that all is spun from their own brain—very rarely anything that has in the least the air of originality. Their compositions are generally commonplace and uninteresting, without character or expression; like those flowery speeches that we sometimes hear, which impress no new ideas upon the mind."

It is said of a celebrated French painter, that a visitor called upon him one day and found him busily engaged

STUDY FOR DECORATIVE FIGURE
By D'Elie Delaunay

making studies for a new work—studies in posture, in facial expression, in drapery, in suggested action. A considerable length of time elapsed, and the visitor again called upon the painter and found him still engaged in the work of making studies for the same composition. The painstaking, plodding

STUDY SQUARED FOR ENLARGEMENT
By Eugene Carman

methods of the painter provoked some exclamation of surprise from the caller. "There is no occasion for wonderment," returned the artist in justification of his multitude of studies. "This is the main part of painting."

Illustrations such as those accompanying this article present no element of novelty to the practiced artist. There are few painters who have essayed creative work who have not well-filled portfolios of sketches of similar character and equal interest. To those, however, unfamiliar with the methods of the studio they give an insight more convincing than words could furnish into the way in which artists have produced the *disjecta membra*, so to speak, of their finished compositions. It would be interesting in the case of some noted picture to reproduce the finished work together with all the studies that entered into its composition. EDGAR CAMERON.

STUDY FOR FIGURE
By Benjamin Constant

STUDY FOR MOUNTED SOLDIER
By Edgar Cameron

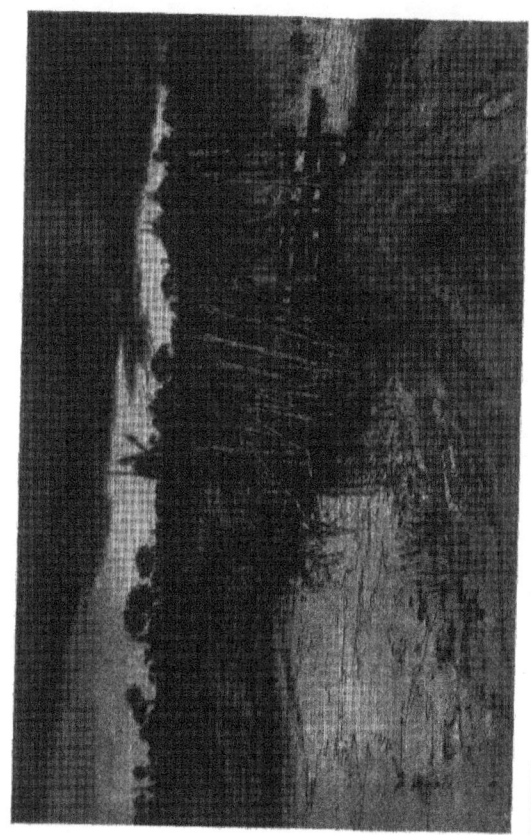

BETWEEN THE GLOAMING AND THE MURK
By Mrs. Mary Nimmo Moran

GALLERY OF ETCHINGS
Plate Sixteen

A UNIQUE TURKISH COFFEE SET

The accompanying illustration represents a Turkish coffee set consisting of a salver, an urn, and four cups and saucers. The decoration is the production of Mrs. Ruth Wilson Tice, a ceramic artist of Minneapolis, who is working along new and original lines. This decoration, which she calls enamel work, is individual with Mrs. Tice, quite her own invention, and has not yet been imitated. Indeed, it would be difficult to imitate.

Though the illustration is a good one, it hardly does justice to the color scheme of the original. The background is gold bronze and

A UNIQUE TURKISH COFFEE SET
By Mrs. Ruth Wilson Tice

has in every way the look of metal. The colors are coral-red and turquoise-blue, but as the blue shows white in the illustration, the subdued beauty of the color effect is lost in the garish prominence of the blue lines of the design.

The cup is a double affair; there is the outer cup, or "zarf," as the Turks call it, and the inner cup, or "fingah." The outer cups look like openwork bronze; the inner ones, of finest white porcelain, bear a flat, conventionalized design in red, blue, and gold. The saucers are very finely and elaborately decorated. The spout of the urn and the upper part of the handle are in plain, dull gold; the contrast between this and the roughened surface of the enamel work is very effective.

An educated Turk, seeing the set, exclaimed over its beauty, and could hardly believe it was not the work or the inception of an Oriental. The decoration as a whole—designs, coloring, and all—embodies not only the art but the religion of the Turks. There are various inscriptions signifying the blessings of Allah; one on the urn being, "Upon this household Allah bring peace."

This set has had generous recognition wherever it has been exhibited, and took the gold medal at Atlanta. It was greatly admired in Cincinnati and was thought worthy of a permanent place in the Fine Art Museum of that city. It still remains in possession of Mrs. Tice, who has not thus far been prevailed upon to part with it except temporarily for the purpose of exhibition.

Charlotte Whitcomb.

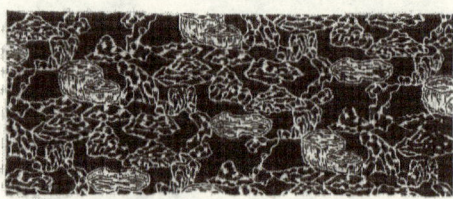

JAPANESE STENCIL
Collection of H. Deakin

RECENT WORK OF ILLUSTRATORS—LOUIS F. BRAUNHOLD

The following cuts are fairly representative of the work of a rising, but comparatively little known, illustrator, Louis F. Braunhold. Mr. Braunhold was born in Chicago in 1854, and was educated at St. Charles, Illinois, in the Fox River Valley. Returning to Chicago in 1869, he adopted art as his profession, working successively in lithography and engraving on wood, and later in pen and wash drawing.

He took up copper plate etching some years ago as an amusement, and has turned out fifty or more plates, many of them of an exceptionally high degree of merit. He has illustrated a dozen volumes of fiction and history, and innumerable pamphlets and brochures. Mr. Braunhold's work is intensely realistic, and his drawings have a spirit and dash indicative of strong feeling and tense, nervous action. He is now engaged on the illustrations for a couple of forthcoming volumes.

PURSUIT AFTER BATTLE OF DONELSON
By Louis F. Hanauhold
From "General Nelson's Scout"
Copyright, 1898, A. C. McClurg & Co.

CLEARING THE FENCE
By Louis F. Hanauhold
From "General Nelson's Scout"
Copyright, 1898, A. C. McClurg & Co.

CHARGE AT MISSIONARY RIDGE.
By Louis F. Braunhold
From "On General Thomas's Staff"
Copyright, 1899, A. C. McClurg & Co.

THE BATTLE OF MILL SPRINGS
By Louis F. Braunhold
From "General Nelson's Scout"
Copyright, 1898, A. C. McClurg & Co.

RECONNOITERING
By Louis F. Baumhold
From "On General Thomas's Staff"
Copyright, 1899, A. C. McClurg & Co.

A WAR INCIDENT
By Louis F. Baumhold
From "General Nelson's Scout"
Copyright, 1898, A. C. McClurg & Co.

CHILDE HASSAM, IMPRESSIONIST

The paintings of Childe Hassam are among the most conspicuous of present-day witnesses that an artist's productions are not faithful transcripts of nature, but bits of nature viewed through a more or less disturbing medium. The painter's art is not mere photography, but photography plus individuality. The artist, to use a figure of speech which may seem trite if not hackneyed, is a lens through which the public catches glimpses of things in the new combinations, the unusual lights, the unique perspectives, resulting from an individual bent of mind; and, to carry the figure farther, upon the clarity, the texture, the convexity, or concavity of the lens depends the worth of the pictures.

DRAWING
By Childe Hassam

Viewed through the eyes of one artist, a given scene or object becomes invested with dignity and meaning, while through the eyes of another the same scene or object is robbed of thought and character. Seen with the aid of one interpreter, it has the witchery of line and color, and with the aid of another it seems paltry, dead, devoid of interest. The scene or object is the same: it is the lens that exalts or debases, magnifies or belittles, suffuses with charm or robs of beauty. The individual element is that which stamps a work with value.

Hassam is impressionistic, after his own fashion idealistic, at times even robust in his sturdy, matter-of-fact treatment. But, whatever his theme or his method, he is strictly individual. He might paint— and his range of subjects is not limited—an odd bit of Brittany architecture or a sleepy nook in Provincetown, a Parisian boulevard or Broadway in New York, the Grand Canal in Venice or the Chicago

Drainage Canal, and however the finished products might differ in other respects, they would all agree in this, that they were Hassam's.

This is not saying that he essays uniqueness, or that he seeks to make capital out of odd selections of subjects or unusual color schemes. He does not. Things impress him in a peculiar way, and he simply

MIDDAY, PONT AVEN
By Childe Hassam

seeks to record his impressions. He recognizes clearly that there is no such thing as absolute realism, and while he tempers the impressions he records on his canvases, and avoids running to the excesses to which some of his fellow-impressionists have been led, he is yet self-reliant and independent enough to paint the world as he sees it, and leave his critics to determine whether his color schemes fit his subjects, and whether his finished works are "according to the masters."

To Hassam the average picture painted for salons and salesrooms is a "Christmas Card," not art. He sees more beauty, more art, in a simple scene daintily dressed in delicate color than in a pretentious composition in which the color possibilities of the palette have been exhausted; and he dreams, though occasionally perhaps despairingly,

IMPROVISATION
By Childe Hassam

of the day when the picture-buying public will have been converted to his views.

"I am often asked," said he recently to the writer, "what determines my selection of subjects, what makes me lean toward impressionism. I do not know. I can only paint as I do and be myself, and I would rather be myself and work out my ideas, my vagaries, if you please, in color, than turn out Christmas cards and have to hire a clerk to attend to orders. I am often asked why I paint with a low-toned, delicate palette. Again I cannot tell. Subjects suggest to me a color scheme and I just paint. Somebody else might see a riot

PEN DRAWING
By Childe Hassam

of color where I see only whites or drabs and buffs. If so, he wouldn't be loyal to himself if he didn't paint the riot, and I wouldn't be true to myself if I did."

To Hassam, therefore, the painter who claims allegiance to a school is a witness of arrested development. On the other hand, the painter who sees for himself and works on his own lines, though he may struggle with the unpopular few, is the artist most worthy of respect and encouragement. He takes no glory in being called an impressionist, nor does he regard it as a reproach or as an indication of personal limitation. Indeed, if asked if he were a realist he would probably say yes — from his standpoint. And he would be right.

"When once the artist has summed up in himself the memories of his apprenticeship, the acquired memories of others, and his own — derived from them, perhaps, but at any rate added to them — you can try him with the following experiment," says that veteran teacher John La Farge. "Take him to ten different places; set him before ten different scenes; ask him to copy what he sees before him. I say to copy so as to make our task of finding him out more easy. All of these so-called copies, which

DRAWING
By Childe Hassam

are really representations, will be stamped in some peculiar way, more or less interesting, according to the value of our artist. And you will recognize at once that they are really ten *copies of his manner of looking at* the thing he copies.

A VILLAGE STREET
By Childe Hassam

"Suppose again that you could persuade ten different artists—I am speaking of craftsmen, that is to say, of people who have already the use of the tools of their trade—ask, persuade these ten men to copy, as I have called it, the same subject in nature, the same landscape; and you will have ten different landscapes, in that you would be able to pick out each one for the way it was done. In short, any person who knew anything about it would recognize, as it were, ten different landscapes."

Hence, La Farge tells his pupils not to be afraid of the word "realism," not to be afraid of indulging the illusion that they are rendering the reality of the things they look at — that they are copying or transcribing. He tells them that they will always give to nature, that is, what is outside of them, their own character. Hassam never took lessons from La Farge, but in a moment of humor might be inclined to accuse the elder artist of appropriating one of his principles.

IN BRITTANY
By Childe Hassam

Hassam, in his brusque way, is prone to inveigh against art schools and art teachers. He regards them as necessary evils that the student should renounce as soon as he has outgrown the swaddling-clothes of his profession, and as regards himself he has been true to his principles. He was born in Boston in 1859 and was educated at the Boston public schools. He began his art studies in his native city, and like many another ambitious student, was led to go to Paris to supplement the instruction received at home. But, as he puts it, his Boston art education was preliminary and his Paris instruction was superfluous.

A short period of the latter sufficed, and whatever of ability the painter has disclosed in his work has been self-developed. He therefore betrays as little perhaps as any of the better known American artists the influence of the masters under whose instruction he sat. Even his impressionism is Hassam's. His peculiar selection of a palette, his mosaic of paint dabs, his freshness, piquancy, spirit, are his own. Of course his favorite methods have their dangers and their limitations. But he sees beauty in what many would reject as unworthy of serious art, and his popularity and the fact that he is many times a medalist sufficiently evidence the fact that he is alert to these dangers and limitations, and knows how to avoid the one and circumvent the other.

THE STAIRCASE
By Childe Hassam

Hassam's name is often associated with pretty bits of Brittany village and rural life, and commonplace but equally pretty scenes in and about Provincetown, where he delights to spend part of his time. Really his interests are broad and his selection of subjects diverse. He paints landscapes and seascapes, picturesque architectural nooks, interiors with up-to-date furnishings and settings. His female faces and figures are especially successful, and his metropolitan street scenes are second to none that have been produced. Indeed, he is one of the very few artists who have found beauty in the teeming busy streets of New York and have produced pictures of street scenes that have value apart from local associations. In these latter he has wisely drawn the line between mere illustrations and finished paintings, and by a process of elimination peculiarly his own, has kept out those details that go to give life and interest to an illustration but militate against a work of art.

Hassam's paintings, whatever be the subject—a village street, a cottage with a flower-dashed garden, a public square, a country

A BRITTANY COTTAGE
By Childe Hassam

church, a lady's boudoir with piano and bric-à-brac, a wind-swept or snow-piled street in the city—open up vistas of beauty that an artist less poetic in temperament and less masterful in technique would scarcely apprehend. He knows how to use high colors to good advantage, but he uses them sparingly. He prefers low tones, but his work is never dull or heavy. Even those paintings in which there is the least suggestion of a high palette scintillate with color, or perhaps one had better say with light and life. There is a *verve*, an alertness, a palpitating life, and withal an element of the winsome in everything he does. Pronounced as are his characteristics, which at times border closely on mannerism, his pictures rarely suggest the monotony of repetition. The man, in a word, has fertility of imagination, which serves as a foil for his favorite color schemes and for his technical peculiarities.

His Brittany cottages, for instance, may present a uniformity of whitish or grayish walls. But these features after all, though essential to a Hassam picture of the district depicted, are subordinate to some central thought or sentiment that is worthy of the painter's art. And so with the prosaic Provincetown scenes and the dainty interiors in which he has been so successful. One feels that the artist is a man of fine sensibilities and delicate perceptions, and that his composition, technique, and choice of colors are a natural outgrowth of his bent of mind.

Hassam has for many years regularly been represented at the leading exhibitions, and art lovers are familiar with his work. In the many canvases he has displayed, his draughtsmanship is uniformly good. His touch is sure and unwavering, his themes are refined and attractive, and his color schemes are harmonious. He has no use for the theatrical, the grewsome, or the tragic. His pictures are more of the nature of idylls in color, and they are prized not less for their inherent grace and beauty than for their fulsome suggestion of pure wholesome life.

The paintings of Hassam are of that peculiar character that makes it difficult to do them justice in reproduction. The accompanying illustrations give but a faint suggestion of the beauty of the originals. The color schemes are too low-toned and delicate, the atmospheric effects are too subtle, the contrasts of light and shade are too indefinitely marked to make the necessary features for a good black-and-white print. In short, the moment one undertakes to transfer a Hassam picture to a printed page the delicate impressionism that constitutes one of its chief charms is lost, and all that is left is a hint of the subject and a general idea of the draughtsmanship.

THE WHITE CHURCH
By Childe Hassam

Hassam has been singularly successful in competitions, and this may be taken as a fair evidence of favorable critical judgment as to his work. He won a medal at Paris in 1889 and one at Munich in 1892. In 1893 he was a medalist at Chicago, in 1894 and in 1899 at Philadelphia, and in 1899 also at Pittsburg. He won prizes of the Boston Art Club in 1890 and in 1895, of the Cleveland Art Association in 1896, and at Pittsburg in 1899. Honors sit lightly upon him, since he is too unpretentious in his life to be puffed up with the pride of success.

He is a close student and a hard worker and one of the most ardent champions of American art. He is a member of Ten American Painters, New York; of the Société National des Beaux Arts, Paris; of the Secession, Munich; of the American Water Color Society; and of the New York Water Color Club. His interests are strictly American, and with his habits of industry and his determination to work out his future on his own line, American art has much to expect from him.

When the eminent French actor, Coquelin, was in America recently, he bought two of Hassam's impressionistic canvases to take back with him to France, declaring at the time of purchase that the artist was the most able impressionist painter in America. The compliment was not ill-advisedly spoken, and Hassam will easily maintain the rank assigned him.

Frederick W. Morton.

COLOR SCHEME AT THE PAN-AMERICAN

It was a hazardous venture, the adoption of a color scheme for the buildings of the Pan-American Exposition, and one for which many artists and architects, with the recollection of former failures of similar enterprises, and the still fresher recollection of the glorious success of the White City of 1893, in which color was eschewed, predicted humiliating results. The verdict, however, of those who have seen the finished work is, that C. Y. Turner, who devised and developed the color scheme, planned more wisely than he knew. The general effect is pleasing and harmonious, and the grounds of the exposition to-day have a distinctive feature never before presented by a similar enterprise.

LIBERTY
Pan-American Exposition

One enters the grounds by the southern entrance and passes through rich, warm colors, which gradually soften into more delicate and refined tones, culminating in cool ivory at the electric tower. The cruder colors are thus massed together, and one leaves them behind on penetrating deeper into the grounds; just as in the process of education one leaves behind him a cruder for a more refined standard of taste.

The whole color scheme of the exposition is primarily a matter of symbolism. As all symbolism implies a liberal draft on imagination, it is safe enough to assume that the average visitor to the exposition will admire the color effects without suspecting their significance. The scheme, which was laboriously worked out by Mr. Turner in his New York studio, is based on the fact that savage races are prone to admire strong colors, and that as education advances, love for the primary colors is supplanted by fondness for softer and more subdued tones. The exposition was designed to show Pan-American progress, and when it was decided to deviate from the conventional practice of painting exposition buildings white or cream, Mr. Turner wisely decided that it would be better to carry out a symbolism of color

CORNER OF PAVILION, MACHINERY BUILDING
Pan-American Exposition

suggestive of progress rather than to use color haphazard throughout the grounds. The general result bears out the wisdom of his decision.

No visitor will contend —and the artist himself as little as any of the visitors—that the plan is not fanciful and in a sense arbitrary. Symbolism aside, there is no sufficient reason why the buildings that happen to be located at the southern end of the grounds should be resplendent in strong primary colors, and those that happened to be farther from the entrance should be toned down till strong colors play but a small part in their decoration. Be this as it may, to the initiated the color scheme is a pleasing conceit, and to the uninitiated it is an harmonious graduation or melting of shades designed to make a striking picture. After all, it is an agreeable effect, and not a more or less hidden meaning that catches the crowd.

The success of this novel experiment in colors is largely due to the skill with which Mr. Turner has done his work. The strong pigments lavished at the southern end of the grounds are in no sense harsh or crude. They have a depth and richness that impart a fine decorative effect. Besides, care has been taken not to allow one primitive color to stand in sharp and disagreeable contrast with other primitive colors. The

MAIN ENTRANCE, TEMPLE OF MUSIC
Pan-American Exposition

TORCH-BEARER, WITH MAGNET
By Philip Martiny
Pan-American Exposition

ELECTRIC TOWER
Pan-American Exposition

assemblage of strong pigments is broken by masses of ivory white that intervene and form a natural medium of transition from one to another of the stronger colors. Were it not for this generous use of white, the color scheme would doubtless seem decidedly garish.

The artist has also judiciously used another means of promoting harmony, by employing a few notes of green in the decoration of every building, adopting a translucent water-green for the purpose. Mr. Turner contends —and his contention is borne out by the history of painting—that green is a refined color and one of comparatively recent use in art. He points to the fact that in early paintings brown is used in place of green, and hence, while it is true that green is one of the colors of the spectrum and was once considered a primary color, it can appropriately and safely be used even among those tones adopted to symbolize the highest development.

The massing of the stronger colors about the entrances of the buildings likewise, and their more sparing use in other parts of the structures, helps materially to enhance the general effect; while the prevailing red of the roofs forms a natural bond of unity throughout the entire color scheme.

Varied and shifting, therefore, as are the colors, one can scarcely say that they are kaleidoscopic. Setting aside the idea typified as the recreation of the sentimental, the eye ranges from color to color and finds pleasure mainly for the reason that the whole is harmonious and decorative.

From first to last the aggregation of buildings presents an appearance as attractive as it is unique. One would hardly wish the horticultural building other than orange,

MANUFACTURERS AND LIBERAL ARTS BUILDING
Pan-American Exposition

with details in blue, green, rose, and yellow; or the governmental building other than yellow, with details in primitive colors; or the music hall other than red; or the machinery building other than greenish gray; or the restaurant group other than ivory, with trimmings of green and gold; or the electric tower other than ivory, yellow, gold, and green.

In short, the risk of adopting a scheme of decoration heretofore deemed inadvisable for large structures was boldly met, and while the promoters of the enterprise may not escape all criticism, it must be said that the work has been executed in a most admirable way.

It will be of interest to the public, doubtless, to learn how this

SOUTH ENTRANCE, MACHINERY AND TRANSPORTATION BUILDING
Pan-American Exposition

color scheme was developed in its entirety. Small sketches of the different buildings were secured by Mr. Turner from the various architects, and from these models were made on a scale of one sixteenth of an inch to the foot. These models were then grouped accurately on a platform twelve by sixteen feet in size, so that the artist had before him the entire exposition in miniature.

These toy buildings were then colored on the basis of the idea of progress to be symbolized, and such modifying or softening touches were added as were deemed necessary in the interest of harmony and general effect. Not a few of the models were painted and repainted a number of times in order to obtain the desired result. When the actual work of decorating the buildings on the grounds was begun, therefore, it was a mere matter of following carefully the miniature exposition turned out from the New York studio of Mr. Turner. Of course more or less touching up was necessary, but this was a matter of detail that gave little trouble to the workmen.

Whatever be the popular verdict, whether the consensus of opinion be in favor of a monochrome scheme, such as was employed at Chicago in 1893, or of a varied, symbolic scheme, such as prevails in the Pan-American, it is to the credit of the promoters of this latter exposition that they had the hardihood to undertake what former exposition managers feared to attempt, and the ability to carry it out to a successful issue.

KATHERINE V. McHENRY.

ELECTRICITY BUILDING
Pan-American Exposition

MORE EXAMPLES OF STUDENT WORK

The following illustrations are the pleasing conceits of a quartet of students. The drawings were made in the regular course of class-work, direction only being given to the efforts by the possible use of the finished pictures in a students' annual. That they are clever, both in conception and in execution, the illustrators of name and fame will readily admit. They are certainly a departure from the cut-and-dried order of pictures presented to the public, and as such the reader will doubtless relish them.

DESIGN FOR "THE INTEGRAL," PUBLISHED BY ARMOUR INSTITUTE OF TECHNOLOGY
By C. H. Wilson, Student at School of Illustration, Chicago

DESIGN FOR "THE INTEGRAL," PUBLISHED BY ARMOUR INSTITUTE OF TECHNOLOGY
By W. B. Johnstone, Student at School of Illustration, Chicago

DESIGN FOR "THE INTEGRAL," PUBLISHED BY ARMOUR INSTITUTE OF TECHNOLOGY
By W. C. Barbour, Student at School of Illustration, Chicago

DESIGN FOR "THE INTEGRAL," PUBLISHED BY ARMOUR INSTITUTE OF TECHNOLOGY
By Irving Mitchell, Student at School of Illustration, Chicago

AT THE JUNGLE DRAMATIC AGENCY
By Hy. Mayer
Courtesy of Dramatic Mirror

HY. MAYER — HUMOROUS CARICATURIST

In the Ryks Museum at Amsterdam is a peculiarly comic composition by A. P. van der Venne, entitled "Fishing for Souls," in which two fleets of rowboats on an inland mere are manned, the one by Catholic prelates in magnificent sacerdotal garments, the other by Protestant clergy in black robes and large felt hats. All are handling fish-lines or scoop-nets with which naked manikins are caught, to be added to the respective folds on the shores. Aside from the artistic excellence of the work as a painting, this panel in its delicious satire may be called one of the forerunners of comic art, which Hogarth and Cruikshank and Nast and Oberländer followed after.

HY. MAYER
From a Photograph

Hy. Mayer is in the first line of succession. Humor is the finest perfection of poetic genius, and Mayer is a wit, a poet, and an artist. Pope tells us, in his "Essay on Criticism," that "wit and judgment often are at strife." In Mayer the union is harmonious.

It is rare that caricature does not have a sting; often it is a barbed arrow, and frequently even it is tipped with poison. Few caricaturists have escaped falling into malice. Take the work of the most famous, of Léandre, Coran d'Ache, Forain, or of Phil May and Harry Furniss, or of Oberländer, Harburger, and Busch. Their *goaks*, as Artemus Ward calls comics, are not always harmless. Not so with Hy. Mayer. His levity has a benign smile, there is nothing spiteful about it. Indeed, this is what makes him a *humorous* caricaturist. The dangerous ground of political cartoons he treads even with unction. In "A Yard of Poppies," a travesty on the yards of pinks, violets, cats, and puppies, which we all know, he presents a line of hilarious members of the people's party, yet with innocent raillery.

VIVE L'ARMÉE
By Hy. Mayer
Courtesy of Black and White

I think, however, that the strong point in his cartoons is the philosophic satire which they contain. During the Dreyfus agitation in France, there appeared his famous cartoon, "Vive l'Armée!" The entire episode of French history is depicted in this cartoon as it could not be done in columns upon columns of editorial writings. It would be the shallowest mind that could ever put upon Mayer's head cap and bells. The sketch, "My Long-lost Brother," Uncle Sam and John Bull embracing each other, with a wink, has been copied all over the world because of its exquisite irony. His series of unconventional statues, which appeared some time ago in a metropolitan magazine, hit off the different men put on the pedestal to perfection. A like series was prepared for a London periodical on English characters.

As in all other things in this present age of novelty, there is noth-

THE ORIGINAL ROOF-GARDEN
By Hy. Mayer
Courtesy of Life

ing new under the sun in caricature. How little that comes forth of wit there is that has claim to true originality. Sterne, stealing the thought from Burton, who had said the same before, says that what we lay claim to as our own is but pouring out of many bottles into one and serving the mixture up in a new shape. So with pictorial burlesque. It is not unreasonable to suppose that the mask of caricature was put on by the early Greeks, and that the sad Heraclitus may sometimes have cracked his sides with mirth, and his frolicsome neighbor, old Democritus, may have wept with laughter. Cruikshank imitated Gilroy, even as Davenport, when he was funny, used to imitate Nast. All the brethren of humorous design ring the changes on the elongated visage, the wide-stretched mouth, the glaring eyes, the skinny leg, the scaramouch action, the extravagant expression, and preternatural proportion, burlesquing camp and senate, church and palace, and holding up to sport the fat, the lean, the tall, the short, the high and low, the rich, the poor, in all the monstrosities and absurdities that make up the farcical view of the great drama of

THE FIRST WAGNER OPERA IN JAPAN
By Hy. Mayer
Courtesy of Life

human life, as seen through the distorted spectacles of the whimsical caricaturist.

Nevertheless we must recognize in Mayer an unusual fecundity of mind and inventiveness. Take his "Worm's Eye Views," of which he has given a wedding, a fire, a picnic, and others; they are all exceptionally good.

We have no right to quarrel with a man of merit because he does not perform impossibilities. Of late years invention has been so whipped and spurred, and incessantly urged upon the full stretch by necessity, that until mankind be endowed with some additional attributes, we may almost venture to say that invention is jaded, if not exhausted. Still men of quick perception offer new combinations of graphic drolling, and fancy in her most freakish moods will continue to hit off to perfection the follies and foibles of mankind.

It is surprising how the unctuous and rollicking "preachments" of our artist vary. There is no repetition of types. In "A Risquée Situation," each facial expression tells its own story of inward thought. Mayer never, by the way, uses models, and with his thousands of sketches, he never draws two faces alike.

Mayer was born in Germany, lived in England, was educated again in Germany, and traveled all over the world; hence his cosmopolitan versatility. The synthetic interpretation of every race and condition of men is fairly within his grasp. With succinct drollery he gives an astounding variety of quips and quirks.

Artistically considered we must rank the work before us of the highest merit. There is more

A YARD OF POPPIES
By Hy. Mayer

than a ridiculous presentation of subjects, serious or otherwise. Arsène Alexandre defines German humor as "A peculiar inventiveness, a turn of wit, at the same time ingenious and grotesque, unex-

SOCIETY CARTOON
By Hy. Mayer
Courtesy of Life

pected and full of straightforwardness." As such Mayer's humor is German. His work is, however, French in its graceful lines with the indefinable accent of daintiness which we find in Cherot or Kaemerer, *vide* the "Chinese Musicians," or the illustrations to his forthcoming "Adventures of a Japanese Doll," or his animal drawings. In his "A Trip to Toyland," as well as in the writing of the jokes

ILLUSTRATION FOR "ADVENTURES OF A JAPANESE DOLL."
By Hy. Mayer

ILLUSTRATION FOR "A TRIP TO TOYLAND"
By Hy. Mayer

CARTOON
By Hy. Mayer
Courtesy of New York Herald

which he illustrates, he further declares a facile pen; in fact, this "Trip to Toyland" is one of the best children's books that has for a long time come from the press. The mirth-inspiring school of art, with never-flagging pencil, has covered enough *charta pura* to placard the walls of China, and etched as much copper as would have sheathed the merchant marine of the world, and to be ranked among the first is Henry Mayer.

Some one has said that the artist or writer who can supply a pleasant thought or excite a smile in the common run of experience is a public benefactor. Measured by this canon of judgment, Mayer is a public benefactor. The depressing, the tragic, the cynical, the sarcastic, the simply prosaic in life, needs the leaven of the humorous that men like Mayer furnish. The caricature that stoops to cruelty or meanness may properly be reprehended; but a laugh hurts nobody, and he would be a harsh critic who would put humor under ban in pictorial art. The popularity of the comic papers is an evidence of the public verdict as regards this class of work; and when all the pros and cons are considered, the verdict of the masses is not to be overlooked or contemned.

DAVID C. PREYER.

CHINESE MUSICIANS
By Hy. Mayer
Courtesy of Pall Mall Magazine

LA CIGALE
By Frank Eugene

AMERICAN PICTORIAL PHOTOGRAPHY AT GLASGOW

The exhibition of pictorial photography is one of the most interesting features of the Glasgow Exposition, and the American display, inconspicuous as it is in point of numbers, probably ranks higher than that of any other nation. Pictorial photography, the use of the camera for the production of photographs with a distinct picture value, is a comparatively young art, and the seventy odd prints shown at the exposition are sufficient witness that Americans have made wonderful progress in transforming the formal and crude prints of a few years ago into pictures that merit the name of art works.

This is not spoken in depreciation of the work of English and Continental photographers. It is but a word of appreciation and praise where appreciation and praise are due. Neatly and appropriately framed, and hung with a fair regard for the requirements of display, the American pictures command attention alike by the wide range of subjects treated and by the delicate and finished character of the work.

They are for the most part pictures that give evidence of maturity of thought and definiteness of purpose. It has been the fashion with artists in all lines of work to name their nondescript productions, for lack of a better word, "studies," and among the American prints at Glasgow these so-called studies are conspicuous by their absence. Indeed, it should be said in justice that the exhibition of prints in its entirety betrays the artist rather than the amateur.

"BLESSED ART THOU AMONG WOMEN"
By Gertrude Käsebier

This exhibition at Glasgow is significant. It is the first time in the history of great expositions that pictorial photography has received anything like the recognition it merited or has even been accorded scant representation. In all the well-known national and international exhibitions, painting, sculpture, etching, engraving, designing for all sorts of textiles and fabrics, in fact, almost every form of art imaginable has been given a place of honor, while photography, which has almost limitless possibilities as a producer of artistic results, has either been overlooked or barred. The recognition given to pictorial photography at Glasgow is due primarily to the wise judgment and enthusiastic enterprise of J. Craig Annan.

Mr. Annan pointed out to the promoters of the exposition that pictorial photography had heretofore been injudiciously slighted. He advocated the desirability of making a place in the art section for a display of that class of photographic work which, by virtue of its pictorial qualities and its nicety of finish, could legitimately be placed in the category of art productions. He even volunteered to secure contributions, and in a sense engineer the exhibition, and his sound argument and his generous tender of assistance resulted in nothing less than in giving photography a new status. He himself traveled

THE DYING FIRE
By C. Yarnall Abbott

all over Europe and elicited the interest of every nation that had essayed to make photography the handmaid of genuine art, and he experienced little trouble in securing worthy contributions from European studios.

The work of securing adequate representation from America had to be delegated to a trusted assistant, and was put in the hands of Alfred Stieglitz. The task of suitably representing the United States at the exposition was not an easy one. The number of frames allotted to America was, approximately, seventy-five. It was further desired to make the collection as representative as possible of the

American school in every phase of pictorial photographic work, and to exclude no artist whose submitted prints met the requirements of the competition. Mr. Stieglitz's position, therefore, was one of no little delicacy, since his judgment might lay him open to the charge of discrimination. Whether he has incurred such charges is not here to the purpose. Suffice it to say, that he selected and sent to the exposition the requisite number of prints, all of admirable quality and representative of the work of thirty American photographers who have acquired for themselves an enviable reputation.

TELEGRAPH POLES
By Clarence H. White

Six artists are represented by five prints each, the other sending from one to four. Many of the pictures now on exhibition at Glasgow are familiar to the American public interested in this class of work, since the prints were selected so as to cover the seventeen years, 1883 to 1900 inclusive, during which pictorial photography has risen to its present state. The American exhibit, therefore, is rather retrospective than new, many of the pictures having already been displayed in American salons. Nothing but picked prints were accepted, and consequently it would be difficult to find a collection of seventy odd photographs more perfect in every respect than the ones sent to Glasgow.

Mrs. Gertrude Käsebier, of New York, sends her charming prints, "The Manger" and "Blessed Art Thou Among Women," together with a "Decorative Panel," "Fruits of the Earth," and "A Portrait." Those familiar with Mrs. Käsebier's work will easily recognize these as among her finest productions. Among the pictures sent by Frank Eugene, of New York, are his remarkable portrait of Mr. Stieglitz,

ZITKALA-SA
By Joseph T. Keiley

ARTISTIC PHOTOGRAPHY
Plate Twelve

his "Adam and Eve," and his striking "La Cigale," which is one of the most admired prints in the collection. Clarence H. White, of Newark, Ohio, contributes among others "Telegraph Poles," in which the camera has invested an exceedingly tame and prosaic scene with a decided poetic charm. His "Spring" and "Laetitia Felix" are equally interesting in point both of subject and of execution.

Mr. Stieglitz himself has no need to apologize for sending five of his own prints, since "The Net Mender," "Winter—Fifth Avenue,"

IN THE FOLD
By Henry Troth

"Scurrying Home," "Watching for the Return," and "A Decorative Panel" are all photographs of a fine degree of excellence. Readers of BRUSH AND PENCIL have already had a fine reproduction of "Scurrying Home" presented to them. They will also remember "Bad News" by Edmund Stirling, of Philadelphia, in which the sorrowful motive of the picture is admirably worked out.

Of Joseph Keiley's prints, "Zitkala-Sa" is here regarded as one of the most interesting, it being a portrait of what to the English public is a unique type. "The Erlking," "The Rising Moon," and "A Study in Flesh Tones" are, however, all equally good in pictorial excellence. The same may be said of Eduard J. Steichen's three landscapes, and his admirable portrait of himself is a fine illustration of well-executed photographic work. So are "Vesper Bells" and "The Dying Day," by Rudolf Eickemeyer, Jr., of Yonkers, New York.

Among the daintiest and most finely suggestive of the prints exhibited are "Clytie," "A Nocturne," and "Landscape," by William B. Dyer, of Chicago. These are all new prints, and are among the best that Mr. Dyer has produced. Zaida Ben Yusef, of New York, sends a couple of excellent portraits and "Odor of Pomegranates," and Rose Clark and Elizabeth Flint Wade, of Buffalo, New York, contribute three prints, two of which I have seen reproduced in the pages of BRUSH AND PENCIL.

Among the other exhibitors—to give a detailed list of titles of prints would scarcely be of interest to the reader—are Eva L. Watson, Philadelphia; Charles I. Berg, New York; W. B. Post, Fryeburg, Maine; Frances B. Johnston, Washington; John E. Dumont, Rochester, New York; Mathilde Weil, Philadelphia; R. S. Redfield, Philadelphia; Emilie Clarkson, Potsdam, New York; Prescott Adamson, Philadelphia; E. Lee Ferguson, Washington; H. Troth, Philadelphia; Mary R. Stanbery, Zanesville, Ohio; John G. Bullock, Philadelphia; T. M. Edmiston, Newark, Ohio; and Mary Devins and F. H. Day, of Boston. These will all be recognized as the names of artists prominent in the coterie that have done so much in America to develop pictorial photography, and when it is taken into consideration that only picked prints of the best productions of these workers have been sent to Glasgow, the reader will have a fair idea of the high degree of excellence that obtains in the exhibition.

The pictorial photographers of America have little need of fulsome praise. They certainly hold their own in this initial exposition display, and the general verdict here is, that the Old World photographers, who have devoted their attention to the lifting up of photography from a more or less barren mechanical process to one of the accepted media of artistic expression, have need to look with jealous eye on the work of their transatlantic confrères.

More important, however, than any consideration of relative merit is the fact that here in Glasgow pictorial photography for the first time takes rank with the allied arts, and one may confidently expect that hereafter the great expositions of the world will be deemed incomplete without suitable exhibits of the higher types of photographic work.

Glasgow, Scotland. ALLAN C. MACKENZIE.

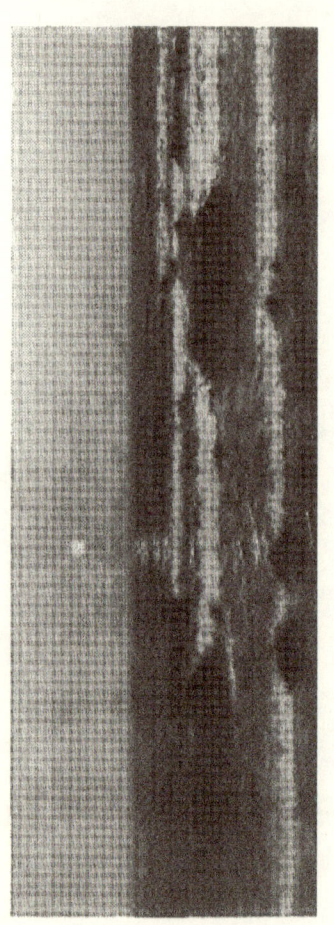

BRUSH AND PENCIL

EDGAR CAMERON, PAINTER

Easily earned reputations and quick successes are generally acquired through specialization. The man who applies all his energies to the study of one subject must gain a more complete knowledge of it than one who divides his attention among several. The painter who thus restricts himself to one class of subjects and who develops a system of painting, produces work which is readily recognized, and he soon becomes known as a painter of whatever line of subjects he has chosen. But when he has played the same tune with slight variations many times, when, in a word, he has ceased to study and to search, he becomes perfunctory and his paintings become articles of commerce rather than works of art. Then, tastes change and new art movements result from these changes in the direction of the thought of the world, and the artist who is no longer capable of receiving new impressions and of giving expression to them becomes a mere "landmark of arrested development."

EDGAR CAMERON
From a Photograph

Edgar Cameron has been exhibiting his paintings publicly since 1888, when his first picture was shown in the Paris Salon. Each year he displays works in the Chicago exhibitions which differ in character and usually in subject from those he has previously shown. There is enough of a family resemblance between them to indicate a common parentage, but in all there are distinctive characteristics which are not the result of a studied determination on the part of the artist to avoid repetitions, but of a policy always to paint what interests him and offers new problems. The result has been that he has made steady progress and has gained in scope as well as in technical ability.

Cameron's picture, "In the Studio," showed good draftsmanship,

DECORATIVE PANEL.
By Edgar Cameron

and was well painted, but betrayed clearly that the painter was still full of the ideas which he had acquired in a serious course of academical training. It was not until two years later, when chance led him to paint some military subjects, that he began to give expression to his own personality. He had just returned from Paris and among other work which he brought with him was a copy made in the Luxembourg Museum of Aimé Morot's "Battle of Reichoffen." This came to the notice of E. C. Moderwell, formerly major of the Twelfth Ohio Cavalry, who in one engagement near Marion, Virginia, received two wounds, had his horse shot from under him at the head of a charge, and was taken prisoner. Mr. Moderwell gave the young artist his first important commission—to paint a picture of the charge which proved so eventful to him. This picture, which was a large one, was composed from descriptions of several of the participants in the fight, with the aid of photographs of the locality where the battle took place, war-time photographs of several of the officers engaged, and studies of landscape, horses, and figures made by the artist.

The interest which he had taken in this work led the artist to paint another military subject, "The Stragglers," which was shown at the exhibition of the Chicago Society of Artists and was burned on the night following the opening. The fire, which destroyed the entire

DECORATIVE PANEL.
By Edgar Cameron

collection, was a severe blow to all of the artists represented, but with more spirit than reflection they decided to hold another exhibition a month later. Cameron found that of this time it was possible to

GRAY NOVEMBER
By Edgar Cameron

devote but sixteen days to painting a picture and decided to repaint "The Stragglers." It was painted larger in size, and some changes were made in the composition. It was completed on time and an Honorable Mention was awarded to it, in the Yerkes prize competition. The higher prizes were awarded to works which had not been completed in time for the first exhibition.

In 1892 Chicago was in the midst of preparations for the World's Fair, and Cameron, along with some of the other young artists of the city, found congenial employment as assistants to some of the Eastern artists who had been given commissions for mural decorations for the buildings of the Exposition. Cameron worked with Robert Reid on the dome in the Manufactures and Liberal Arts building, and with Walter McEwen on large tympana for the same structure. He was also employed on less important work and was given a commission to execute two panels, seven by seventy feet, for the interior of the Transportation building.

BANKS OF THE SEINE
By Edgar Cameron

Some time previous to this he had undertaken the writing of a weekly art review for a leading Chicago newspaper. This was a sort of work which proved most agreeable to him. It gave him opportunities for continued study in many directions and, affording a source of revenue, saved him from the necessity of teaching or painting "pot-boilers," which were the only alternatives Chicago presented at that time to most of those who were struggling to follow an artistic career. During the six months which followed the opening of the Exposition there was enough art to be seen to require almost daily articles, and during this period copy pages took the place of canvas and pencils that of brushes.

At the close of the World's Fair, Cameron returned to Paris for three years. Two winters were spent in study in the schools, and the remainder of the time was devoted to painting pictures. A part of the time was spent in painting landscapes along the Seine and in the forest of Fontainebleau. One summer was spent in the fishing village of Étaples, on the coast of the Channel, and the last winter was occupied in the painting of a large, religious subject, "The Youth of Christ."

This picture, which is the most important of the canvases brought back from Europe and shown as a collection at a Chicago gallery, is an idealistic creation depicting the boy Jesus at a period of his life of which the Bible gives no record. He is represented standing at the bench in Joseph's carpenter shop, as if in the midst of his worldly occupations his thoughts had turned to the career for which he was preordained. There appears before him the vision of a spectral cross, from which a dim light is reflected on the figure, robed in a single tunic of white. In the soulful expression of the face and the suggested movement of the figure there is a sentiment of suppressed emotion forcefully depicted. The rude bench, the primitive tools, and the curled shavings scattered on the floor show a conscientious completeness which bespeaks the reverent feeling in which the picture was conceived. The words of St. Luke, "And Jesus increased in wisdom and stat-

A FRIEND THROUGH INTEREST
By Edgar Cameron

OLD AGE
By Edgar Cameron

ure and in favor with God and man," seem to have suggested the subject. This painting is now in the Union League Club, Chicago.

Among the other pictures which were exhibited at this time were some landscapes which were charming for their poetic feeling and completeness of the delicate detail.

Most of Mr. Cameron's landscapes are composed and executed in

LEDA
By Edgar Cameron

such a way that the attention is focused near the foreground—the portion of a landscape which is most often slighted. This may result from a temperamental interest which the artist takes in his immediate surroundings. In his work he has also never shown a disposition to avoid difficulties, but seems rather to take delight in them. His "Gray November" is an example. The foreground is an abandoned lot of ground overgrown with flowers, weeds, and shrubbery which has taken on the yellows and browns of autumn. It is painted carefully, the plants are drawn with an accuracy which permits their identification. Beyond are groups of trees simply and broadly treated which mark the distance except a glance of the roofs of a village and an effective gray sky.

Two pictures of interiors with old women seated by lonely fireplaces, shown in the same collection, have something of the quiet melancholy which is characteristic of the works of Israels and some of

THE YOUTH OF CHRIST
By Edgar Cameron

the other modern Dutch painters. They are low-toned color harmonies in keeping with the character of their subjects. They were painted while the artist was living among the poor fisher folk and peasants in France, and he seems to have been deeply impressed with the hopeless poverty of their existence.

CARMEN
By Edgar Cameron

The next important group of paintings by Cameron showed a decided change, both of manner and of feeling. They were full of light and color, and cheerful in subject. They were the result of a summer and early autumn spent in St. Joseph, Michigan. They were chiefly landscapes, bright country roadways, views of the beach of Lake Michigan, and the river. Two night scenes alone had something of the sentiment of his earlier work. One figure subject was the result of the idea that it is possible to make an artistic painting and at the same time embody a pleasing subject which might appeal to the public which demands a story. It was called "A Friend Through Interest," and showed a lane with a picturesque old apple-tree hanging over a fence and a bridge in the foreground which in itself would have made an interesting subject. The story is added by the figure of a young woman carrying a pail of milk, with a half-grown cat sidling beside her and displaying its concern for a prospect of a share of the contents of the pail.

Two years ago Mr. Cameron exhibited two pictures, each displaying study in new directions. One was a charming and poetic conception of Leda. The lightly draped figure of the young woman is shown in a secluded clearing in a wood by the side of a quiet pool where "saw the swan his neck of arched snow and oared himself along with majesty." The other picture was an interior of a glass factory with half-nude figures of the blowers at work in the glow of the furnace. It was a study of contrasting warm and cool lights successfully elaborated. It was sold on the opening night of the exhibition to the "Chicago Woman's Aid Club," which had earnestly taken up the study of labor problems.

Last spring at the Chicago Artist's Exhibition, Mr. Cameron exhibited a landscape, a figure subject and a marine. The marine view was painted from studies made on the ocean the summer before. It was broad and effective in treatment and vigorous in its effect. It showed an expanse of the blue water of mid-ocean agitated by a brisk breeze and a sky full of moving, fleecy clouds. Its title, "The Voiceful Sea," was a fitting one. The picture is now the property of the Arché Club. The other pictures were an evening effect with the figure of a young woman ac-

THE RENDEZVOUS
By Edgar Cameron

companied by a dog walking on a sedgy river bank, and a landscape showing ...e flowery banks of the same river mottled with patches of bright afternoon sunlight and the shadows of trees and the summer residences which lined its banks.

The latest picture which Mr. Cameron has painted is one which demonstrates clearly the value of a varied training in the painting of many subjects. It was a commission for a seasonable subject for Decoration Day and had to be composed to fit unusual proportions of length and breadth. It was intended for reproduction and required an amount of sentiment sufficient to make

A SURPRISE
By Edgar Cameron

it popular with the general public. Two weeks was allowed for its execution.

The subject selected was that of an aged mother with her son's uniform, sword, and other mementoes on a chair opposite her, and a letter in her hand. In the center of the picture was an open fireplace with the fire throwing a faint glow on the surrounding objects. Hanging above the old-fashioned marble mantel was the portrait of the son as he might have appeared in the Civil War period, with a flag draped about the frame. The figure of the woman and the interior, which were typically American and sufficiently picturesque, were found, almost as the artist painted them, in a village about seventy-five miles from Chicago.

Besides producing pictures, Mr. Cameron has found time to take an active part in art matters in other ways. He was vice-president of the Chicago Society of Artists during the period of the World's Fair. He has held four private exhibitions of his work in Chicago, was organizer of a pastel exhibition, and took the initiative in the project of auction sales in which other artists took part. He has acted at various periods as instructor in the Art Academy and the School of Illustration in Chicago. He has written regularly for the press on art topics. Last year he was appointed a member of the International jury of the Paris Exposition, being assigned to Class XII., which included exhibits of photography, photographic materials, and photo-mechanical processes.

Ever since his work on decorations for the World's Fair, Cameron has devoted considerable attention to the subject of mural painting, and has made compositions whenever a possibility for securing such work presented itself.

The fact that he is so well equipped as a draftsman and as a painter has led many of his friends to advise him to choose a line of subjects, but he has persistently refused to do this and holds to the belief that it is not subject so much as the expression of an artist's own personality which makes his work valuable. Without aiming for variety or searching for novelty he has made it a rule to paint such subjects as he found of interest to himself at all times, believing that this is the best way to produce work which will interest others. His early training may be to some extent responsible for this.

He began to draw cartoons and to engrave them on wood when still a schoolboy, and feeling the need of some training in drawing, he attended the Chicago Academy of Design for a short time during two of his summer vacations. After an interval of several years he went to New York to study at the Art Students' League. Although he had not continued to draw he had grown in perception, for within three weeks after he arrived in New York he made a full-length drawing of the Discobolus, which admitted him to the life class. This escape from the "Antique" Mr. Cameron considers a most fortunate circumstance. From the start he was spared from the influences of tradition.

The next year he went to Paris, and after six months in the Julian Academy, too short a time to feel much of the effects of the academical training of Boulanger and Lefebvre, he passed the examination for the École des Beaux Arts, where he entered the studio of Cabanel, who was one of the most liberal of masters. His evenings he spent in modeling in clay at the École des Arts Decoratifs, and his summers in the country studying landscape, chiefly at Barbizon and Grez, where there were several older artists.

After two years in the Beaux Arts he went to Venice with two friends and began his first attempts at picture-making, but did not show any of this work until after his admission to the Salon a year later.

CHARLES M. TOWNE.

PASSING OF A FAMOUS ARTIST, EDWARD MORAN

In the death of Edward Moran, who passed away in his New York studio on June 9th last, America lost one of its ablest and most versatile artists. Coupled with his rare ability as a painter, he had an unusual aptitude for teaching his art, and, perhaps what is equally noteworthy, a genius for work. To him is due primarily the development of his brothers, Thomas and Peter, and also of the younger generation of Morans, Percy and Leon, all of whom have acquired enviable reputations.

In a broader sense, he exerted a deep influence on many another American artist, since he was one of the earliest and stanchest members of that school to which Inness and Wyant belonged, and which did so much to give distinctiveness and character to American art. Throughout his long career his work held its own in all the changes of taste and fashion, and he maintained his popularity to the end. Indeed, he had scarcely laid down his brush on finishing his last commission, a painting for Mr. Dewitt of Oswego, when he succumbed to the disease which had made him more or less an invalid for a year.

Opinions may differ as to his rank, but Mr. Moran, by common acceptance, was a universal genius as a painter. His range of subjects was broad, and he used with equal facility as mediums of expression oils, water-colors, and pastel. Few artists have painted more charming landscapes or better cattle pieces, and none, perhaps, have surpassed him as a painter of marines. It is as a painter of seascapes, doubtless, that he will live in fame.

Mr. Moran's life, savoring as largely as it did of the drudgery of the studio, was not without its touch of romance, that will be appreciated by all artists who have had forced upon them the irony incident to successful achievement. He was born at Bolton, Lancashire, England, August 19, 1839, coming with his family to Philadelphia at the age of fifteen, and later settling in Maryland. There for upward of seven years he worked at a power loom. His love of art, however, which had first evinced itself in boyhood in an ability to cut figures from paper, and later in clever sketches which he drew on the cloth as it came from his loom, determined the young man to follow an artistic career.

So one day he packed his personal belongings and set out on foot for Philadelphia, walking the entire distance. As might have been expected, he, on arriving in the Quaker City, found the necessities of subsistence more imperative than the impulse to make pictures. With art, therefore, as a beacon before him, he first became an em-

OFF SANDY HOOK
By Edward Moran
Collection of Mr. John Miller, New York

AMERICAN PAINTINGS
Plate Twelve

ploye in a cabinet-making establishment, then he worked in a bronzing shop, and finally he took his first lessons in painting—houses.

In these early days of stress he demonstrated the fact that all things come to him who waits and hustles while he waits, the turning point of his life being when he secured an introduction to Paul Webber and James Hamilton, at that time among the best known artists in Philadelphia. He began his artistic career under their guidance and at their instance took a room in Callowhill Street, and opened as modest and perhaps as ill-equipped a studio as ever sufficed the purposes of an aspirant for fame. Ability, patience, time, and industry won the day, and it was not long before he in a sense became the art godfather of his family.

"He taught the rest of us Morans all we know about art and grounded us in the principles we have worked on all our lives," said his brother Thomas Moran recently on his return from the Yellowstone region, where he was sojourning on a sketching tour at the time of Edward's death. "It is scarcely probable that any of us would have been painters had it not been for Edward's encouragement and assistance. Such ability as we had was doubtless latent in us, but he gave us our bent, and such successes as we have attained, we primarily owe to him."

Twenty-five years ago Edward Moran left the city in which he had first obtained recognition and went to New York, where, with occasional visits to London and Paris, he lived to the time of his death. The amount of work he accomplished during the last quarter of a century was enormous, and yet, despite the great output of his studio, he never slighted his canvases or resorted to pot-boiling methods. His work was all true, direct, and sincere.

In a measure he lacked the ideality of his brother Thomas, and was not wooed as was the latter by the grander aspects of nature. His tastes were more pastoral, and his landscapes, therefore, were simpler and less pretentious than his brother's. Indeed, his cattle pictures were a direct outgrowth of this peculiar bent of mind, being due to his love of domestic animals and to the human interest with which he sought to invest his canvases.

As a painter of the sea in its many moods and phases, Edward Moran, it is commonly admitted, had no superior in America. He recognized his forte and fostered his ability in this line. He had an ambition to live in history as a great marine painter, and shortly after his change of residence to New York he outlined for himself a series of historical paintings, which, in a sense, should be a pictorial narrative of the achievements of the American navy. For the execution of this great enterprise he began studiously to prepare himself in every possible way, and he undertook his task, leaving his provisional outline lax enough to permit of changes and additions, but adhering throughout to his fixed purpose.

This most important series was begun twenty years ago, and was finished soon after the close of the war with Spain. It consists of thirteen paintings representing thirteen important epochs in the marine history of the United States. They are: The Ocean; the highway of all nations. Landing of Eric the Red in the new world in 1001. Santa Maria, Nina, and Pinta. Debarkation of Columbus. Midnight mass on the Mississippi over the body of De Soto. Sir Henry Hudson entering New York harbor on September 11, 1609. Embarkation of the Pilgrim Fathers at Southampton on October 5, 1620. First recognition of the American flag by any foreign government in the harbor of Queberon, France, on February 13, 1776. Burning of the United States frigate Philadelphia in the harbor of Tripoli on February 16, 1804. Great Armstrong, brig, engaging the British fleet in the harbor of Fayal on September 26, 1814. Iron vs. Wood; the sinking of the United States steamship Cumberland by the Merrimac in Hampton Roads. The white squadron's farewell salute to the body of Captain John Ericsson in New York harbor on August 25, 1890. The return of the conquerors, typifying the victory of the navy in the war with Spain.

Many art lovers will doubtless see more merit in Mr. Moran's simpler canvases, but this is largely a matter of taste. The artist was a severe critic of his own work and it remains for time to prove whether his judgment as regards his own achievements was not sound.

Among Mr. Moran's best known and most highly prized paintings are his "Return of the Fishers," "The White Cliffs of Albion," "New York Harbor," and "The Statue of Liberty on the Day of Unveiling," the latter of which was sold to Mr. Drexel, of Philadelphia, for ten thousand dollars. Throughout his career, Mr. Moran was deeply interested in organizations devoted to the advancement of his art. He was a charter member and at one time vice-president of the Lotus Club, a member of the American Water Color Society, an associate of the National Academy of Design, and a member of the London Water Color Society.   HUGH W. COLEMAN.

RECENT WORK OF ILLUSTRATORS— CHARLES ROBINSON

The following pictures are fairly indicative of the work of one of the younger English decorative illustrators, Charles Robinson. He is one of the most charming of artists for children, combining delicacy of thought and a wealth of invention. He shows a quaint and sometimes weird fancy, a love of fantastic architecture and a fearlessness in the use of strong outlines and suggestive white spaces. His drawings are well worth the study of those who find delight in poetic conceits gracefully expressed.

THE ARGONAUTS
By Charles Robinson
From "The True Annals of Fairy Land"
The Macmillan Company, Publishers

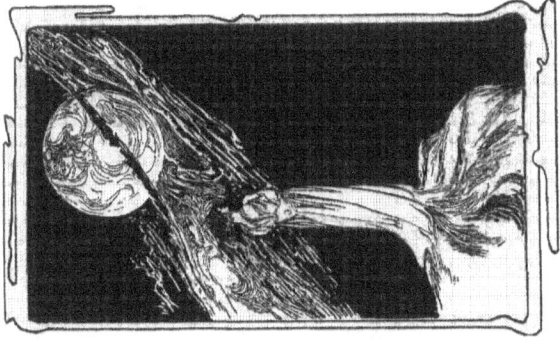

THE SOARING LARK
By Charles Robinson
From "The True Annals of Fairy Land"
The Macmillan Company, Publishers

THE STANDING STONES
By Charles Robinson
From "The True Annals of Fairy Land"
The Macmillan Company, Publishers

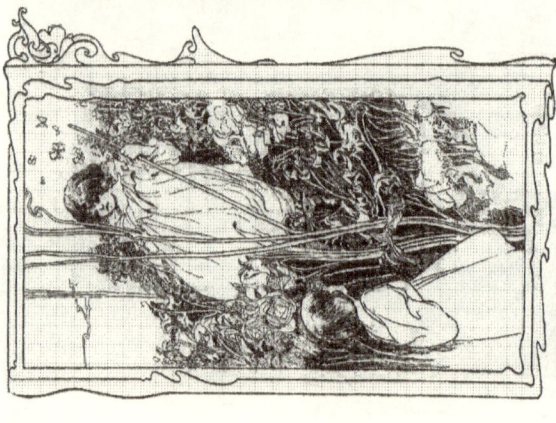

"ART THOU COME TO VISIT US?"
By Charles Robinson
From "The True Annals of Fairy Land"
The Macmillan Company, Publishers

THE BEAUTIFUL GOOSE
By Charles Robinson
From "The True Annals of Fairy Land"
The Macmillan Company, Publishers

LITTLE SNOW WHITE
By Charles Robinson
From "The True Annals of Fairy Land"
The Macmillan Company, Publishers

THE CHILDREN OF LIR
By Charles Robinson
From "The True Annals of Fairy Land"
The Macmillan Company, Publishers

ON THE GLASS MOUNTAIN
By Charles Robinson
From "The True Annals of Fairy Land"
The Macmillan Company, Publishers

MODELING FROM LIFE
By Mary M. Naughton and Lena Qualley

ART EDUCATION IN AMERICA[*]

"A great change has taken place in public sentiment. The arts are no longer regarded as comparatively unimportant to our national growth and dignity, and an ever-increasing enthusiasm has replaced languid interest or indifference. Our great cities have their museums, their art schools, and lectures; our colleges, their art professors and their collections of casts and pictures; and our libraries, their multiplicity of books upon artistic subjects, whose circulation equals, if it does not surpass, that of books on other topics. A desire to keep up with the times in art matters, as in all else, seems to have taken possession of us, and the names and works of Ruskin, Hamerton, Charles Blanc, and Lübke are as familiar to us as to our European brethren."

These words were written twenty years ago by one of the closest observers of American art and art conditions. They are, of course, the words of an enthusiast,

WATER-COLOR FROM STILL LIFE
By Clarence Bodine

[*]Illustrations by students.

but they fairly express the birth of a new era in our national life. He, however, would have been deemed a bold prophet who would have predicted two decades ago the deeper and more widespread

STUDY IN OIL FROM LIFE
By Mabel Packard

interest that now obtains in this country in all forms of fine art, or the increased and improved facilities now offered to students for developing their abilities, or the magnificent results now evidenced in American art exhibitions.

WATER-COLOR FROM CAST
By Katherine Newbury

CHARCOAL DRAWING FROM CAST
By Cora B. Shinkle

Never was love of art and pride in American achievement so manifest as at the present time. Never were such opportunities offered to the general public for indulging its tastes. Never were American institutions better equipped for developing native talent. The student classes are awake to their privileges, and as a consequence the better class art schools of this country show an annual increment in the matter of enrollment. All educational methods in a large measure are the result of experiment, and this awakened interest in art, this marked influx of students to the art schools, brings its new problems and its new duties and responsibilities to teachers and directors alike.

To what extent shall old methods be followed or new methods be countenanced? How best shall the pressing needs of the present day be met? On what lines shall courses of study be cast so that students may receive the greatest possible benefit from the instruction given them? In what way shall those into whose hands naturally falls the guidance of youth best foster the love

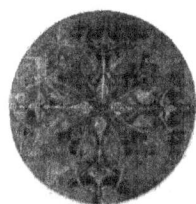

DECORATIVE CIRCLE
By Mrs. Evelyn Beachey

DECORATIVE DESIGN
By Flora H. Woods

of art, stimulate effort toward worthy attainment, and perpetuate the movement, begun a generation or more ago, as stated in the foregoing quotation, and bring it to its full fruition? These are all vital questions, the earnest of many another that might be asked, and upon the conclusions reached by teachers depends the worth of art schools as a factor in higher education. A word of suggestion, the result of wide experience, may not be untimely.

ED.

The career of the successful artist, like that of all other successful men, depends upon various elements, chief among them, the character of the man himself, his general attainments, and his professional accomplishments. It is this last element with which the art school must chiefly concern itself, although the wise plan would contemplate such an arrangement of conditions as would favor also the development of character and the increase of general attainments.

In a certain sense it may be said that when you have provided a good teacher, a good model, and a good light, you have all the essentials for art study which the world affords. But to these essentials may be added many collateral advantages; and it is found that an art school, like an individual, takes on character and maturity by course of time.

DESIGN FOR RUG
By Edith Jeffrey

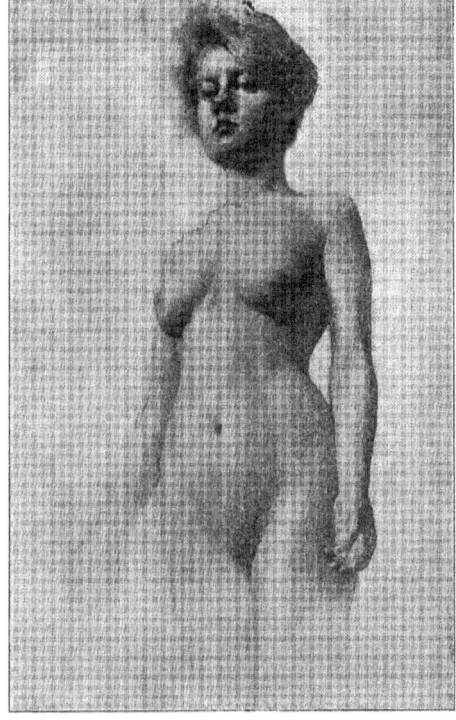

CHARCOAL STUDY FROM LIFE
By Louise Perrett

In American art schools it must be clearly recognized that by no means all the students contemplate the profession of an artist, but many will become illustrators and teachers. The problem is so to arrange conditions that a student with no professional preparation shall in three or four years acquire good technical methods, and open the door to progress in his profession.

By almost universal consent the basis of the practice of art is the

DECORATIVE DESIGNS
Book Covers by Anna M. Lessman and Nell W. Hagny
Wall-Paper Patterns by Helene E. Warder and M. Maude Knox

study of the human head and figure, and this not for any mysterious reason, but because they are full of subtile line and color, are easily obtained, and are endless in variety, yet with sufficient constancy to make correction possible. The elementary student, therefore, should begin at once to study the figure, probably at first from fragments of the antique, as being simpler and easier than life. Probably half the day is enough for such severe drawing, and the other half may be given particularly to sketches of the figure at rest and in action.

At the same time elementary perspective should be begun, which

STUDIES IN OIL FROM LIFE
By Lena Qualley, Ethel L. Coe, Walter Rowe, and Louise Neal

is best done by the drawing of geometrical solids from nature and from memory. This is of decided importance, since no free-hand drawing can be made which does not involve perspective, and ignorance of it is similar to bad spelling and bad English in writing or speaking. It is surprising how many pretty good artists are unwilling to give a brief period of study to this grammatical point, but the best do not neglect it. The student pursues his drawing of antique through successive stages until he can manage the whole figure in full light-and-shade, and by this time he should have access to the nude figure a part of the time, so as to understand what the antique means.

With regard to technical handling, mediums, and the like, there is a considerable range of choice, and it may be set down as certain that the teacher must be allowed to use those which he prefers. No artist or drawing teacher worthy of the name will accept dictation upon these points, and in general the only way to manage a large art school, or, I suspect, any educational institution, is to choose able teachers, and allow them to work out their own specialties freely, co-ordinating the different classes as may be possible.

PEN AND INK SKETCH
By A. Belassa

A moderate course of study of artistic anatomy, with strict reference to the living model, may well be taken rather early, and ought to be accomplished in much less than a year. Experience goes to show that in an art school it is scarcely feasible for students to begin to use color (except in a sketch class, where they work at will) until they can draw well enough to put ordinary still-life objects in place for themselves, that is, probably about the time they take up the full figure in antique, with limited nude study.

Painting in oil or water-colors from still-life objects and draperies is a proper preparation for painting from life. Meanwhile careful drawing from the nude figure and head goes on, and most teachers think that modeling in clay is also a useful exercise for the artist. Finally the student attains to painting in full from the figure and the costumed model with accessories.

For simplicity one important element has been omitted thus far, that of original composition. From the beginning a student should practice composition or picture-making, even in a rude way, in the classes of illustration and of composition. Memory drawing should be stimulated by the assignment of subjects for illustration in which the student relies upon material accumulated in his studies elsewhere.

PEN AND INK SKETCH
By N. P. W. Swanson

He should learn to present a given subject in agreeable form with regard to line, arrangement, and balance of light-and-shade. This study gradually develops until it eventuates in a completed picture.

STUDY IN OIL FROM LIFE
By Daisy Dunton

Specialists in illustration, of course, must learn the peculiar mediums and processes of their art. For those who intend to become teachers it is necessary to provide special pedagogic instruction.

Thus far we have been speaking of actual practice alone, but for the highest advantage the student must have access to lectures upon history, theory, and practice of art by the most competent authorities, must enjoy the use of an art library containing not only books but reproductions of great masterpieces of art, and must have opportunity to visit permanent and passing collections of paintings of the highest quality.

The most comprehensive schools embrace departments, not only of drawing, painting, and modeling, but also of decorative designing and architecture, and it is found that the interaction between what is called fine art and industrial or applied art is wholesome and beneficial on both sides. Strictly speaking, the term "art school" is a misnomer, because art in the sense in which it is common to literature, music, painting, and sculpture cannot be taught otherwise than by the general cultivation of the individual. Such terms, therefore, as "school of art practice," or "school of drawing and painting," etc., are preferred by the best authorities, except for brevity. It would be well if it were possible for schools of art practice to embrace also the study of poetry, language, history, and mythology, but the art courses are too short to permit of this, and the student must be relied upon to devote attention to these subjects elsewhere.

W. M. R. FRENCH,
Director of the Art Institute of Chicago.

CRAYON SKETCHES
By N. P. W. Swanson and Alice Cleaver

PECONIC, LONG ISLAND
By J. W. Casilear

AN AMERICAN PATRON OF AMERICAN ART

The caption of this article is significant. It is the plaint of American artists—and it is one well founded in fact—that American collectors of paintings, be they individuals or institutions, are prone to slight, if not condemn, home talent, and spend their money freely for alien works, which are often cheap and meretricious, but which have about them somewhere the charm of a foreign name. For thirty years or more it seems to have been an unwritten law among the picture-buying public of this country that there was no art but foreign art, and the business instincts of the dealers have led them to be willing apostles of the new creed.

The result is that American galleries, for the most part, are congested with Old World products, while equally meritorious, if not superior, paintings by American artists go begging for purchasers. Indeed, many a talented American—witness Whistler, Sargent, Knight, Abbey, McEwen, Alexander—has taken up a foreign residence, as much from policy as from choice; and, being in a sense expatriated, they have found favor with American collectors which they never would have enjoyed had they remained at home and turned out the same works from New York, Philadelphia, or Chicago studios.

In this craze for the works of foreign painters, it is refreshing to find a collector like Mr. Frederick S. Gibbs, of New York, who buys pictures for the delight he takes in them, who can see merit in a canvas without first looking for the name in the corner of it, and who, in consequence, has for more than a quarter of a century been one of the most generous patrons of home talent found among American collectors.

His collection now numbers two hundred and twenty paintings, representing about one hundred and thirty different artists. In 1899 Mr. Gibbs published a catalogue of his collection, at which time he had one hundred and eighty paintings, representing one hundred and twenty-five artists, a large majority of whom were Americans. Since the publication of his catalogue, Mr. Gibbs has sold fifty-one of his collection of paintings and has replaced them with ninety-one other canvases, still adhering to his original policy of being a patron of American art.

A SIP BY THE WAY
By James M. Hart

In his collection, as it now stands, there are fourteen canvases by J. Francis Murphy, six by Inness, six by Wyant, and five by Robert C. Minor. Among other American artists represented by recent purchases are H. W. Ranger, R. M. Shurtleff, Frank de Haven, Leonard Ochtman, Julian Rix, Louis Paul Dessar, E. L. Henry, Alfred C. Howland, J. B. Bristol, Charles Warren Eaton, Edward Gay, Henry Mosler, H. Siddons Mowbray, H. Bolton Jones, H. A. Loop, Kruseman van Elten, Bliss Baker, and many earlier men of wider fame. The paintings by the artists named among Mr. Gibbs's later acquisitions are indicative of the interest the collector takes in present-day American works of merit.

CUPID ASLEEP. By Jacques C. Wagrez

SCENE IN ALGIERS. By Georges Washington

IN THE BARNYARD
By C. V. Turner

To be sure, Mr. Gibbs has a fondness—and who has not?—for certain foreign artists of note, and we find in his collection such names as Corot, Zeim, Pasini, Chelminski, Clays, Tamburini, Rousseau, Herrmann, Rico, Fortuny, Vibert, Marais, Diaz, Berne-Bellecour, Henner, Richet, Van Marcke, and other masters, but despite the liberal sprinkling of foreign works in his collection, Mr. Gibbs's deepest interest is in his American paintings, and he stands to-day distinctively one of the best friends American painters have in New York.

Mr. Gibbs started his collection about thirty years ago, beginning without aim or plan further than to gratify his love of pictorial art, and screening his hobby even from intimate friends. His experience, therefore, was not unlike that of many another collector. Many of his early purchases were graduated by stages from the front to the back of the house and finally into other collections, paintings of higher quality and better character taking their place.

"Painting always had a strong attraction for me," said he to the writer, recently, "and when I joined a club twenty-five years or more ago in which a number of the members were artists, my interests in paintings grew as I began collecting. It is difficult to determine now the exact motives of my choice of paintings in the beginning, but at that time I was willing to be guided in my selection by the judgment of friends whose opinions I respected. Now, I add to my collection for the merit I see in a picture, regardless of the name of the artist, and so I have a delightful personal pleasure in every painting on my walls. All my collections of paintings have been made solely from the standpoint of the collector."

There is, of course, an element of the haphazard in this method of procedure, but the plan is not without its merits. A collection formed in this way is based primarily on the purchaser's love of art. It furnishes a liberal market for the works of rising men of merit. It never palls, since it is constantly subject to the correction of broadening knowledge and maturing taste. It is, further, better for the artist classes that a collector should have a strong but undefined impulse toward art that impels him to buy liberally and weed out as liberally, than that he should invest his money in a few canvases acknowledged to be masterpieces and close his market to newer work of possibly equal value.

Mr. Gibbs is to-day recognized as a connoisseur of what is good in pictures, and surprises artists and critics alike by his excellent judgment. The fact that the first painting he purchased was moved step by step to a rear room on the top floor of his house is not without a certain historical and personal significance. It shows that the collector was actuated at first largely by fancy, that he had a strong feeling for color effects which often determined his purchases, that he was often led to invest in canvases having a vogue only to replace them later with better and truer forms of art.

At first Mr. Gibbs's progress in collecting was slow. It is prob-

THE PASTURE IN THE MEADOWS
By Carleton Wiggins

able that he did not buy more than four pictures a year for the first ten years of his collecting. The habit of buying, however, once formed, grew. Old paintings were removed or disposed of to make room for new arrivals. As the collection increased in number it was enhanced in quality, until it may now be confidently said that Mr. Gibbs's gallery is thoroughly representative of America's best work.

He has, it is true, some paintings of a type that to-day is little prized, but he has also some exceptionally rare canvases. That it was the painting not the price, in other words, that it was personal taste and not hearsay, that determined Mr. Gibbs's purchases is pretty conclusively shown by the fact that he bought an authentic A. H. Wyant for fifteen dollars and moved a costly painting so as to make a permanent place for it in his living-room.

The transformation of Mr. Gibbs's collection is really due to his acquisition of certain excellent examples of the work of Inness, Wyant, Murphy, Minor, and a few other of our better American painters, together with some canvases by foreign landscape painters, which acted as a leaven. In its earlier stages his private gallery was rich in figure painting of the kind that tell a story, the kind, in short, that has been popular in reproductions. But Mr. Gibbs gradually outgrew the merely pictorial, or melodramatic, and by his process of elimination has made room on his walls for a collection of fairly equal value, without sharp or unpleasant discords.

THE EDGE OF THE WOODS
By J. B. C. Corot

This predominance of American canvases impresses one immediately on entering Mr. Gibbs's home. He takes especial pride in his paintings by Inness, Murphy, Wyant, and Minor, these artists being especial favorites. Two of the Inness pictures, "Light Triumphant"

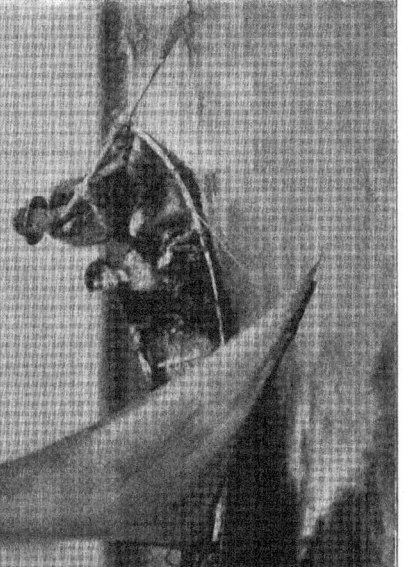

RUNNING FOR HOME
By Francis C. Jones

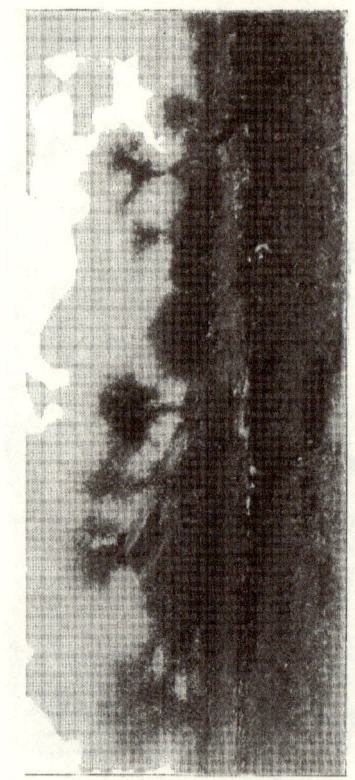

LIGHT TRIUMPHANT
By George Inness

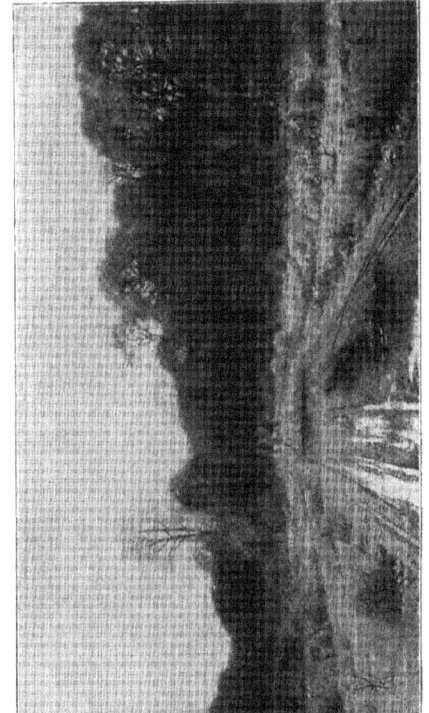

WET DAY IN OCTOBER
By C. Harry Eaton

SUMMER—SUNSHINE AND SHADOW
By George Inness

and "Summer—Sunshine and Shadow," are perhaps more highly prized than any other paintings in the collection. They were formerly owned by Henry Ward Beecher, being purchased by Mr. Gibbs shortly after the death of the great divine. The former of these paintings is a flat stretch of landscape with the horizon lying low on the canvas and the broad expanse of sky a blaze of yellow. In the middle foreground is an old farmhouse standing gable end toward the spectator and a half-dozen or more trees. The latter canvas to many would be the more pleasing. One catches through a nearby grove of trees, under which cattle are resting, a glimpse of distant hills. These paintings, as indeed all the canvases by Inness, are thoroughly representative of that painter's best work.

FLIRTATION
By Percy Moran

The canvases by Wyant and Murphy are equally representative and equally choice. One of the former, "Smugglers' Cave in Jones's Woods," a mere sketch in subdued grays and browns, is interesting partly from the fact that Mr. Gibbs, as already stated, bought it for a mere trifle, and partly from the fact that this particular picture, which was painted about 1869, is so unlike Wyant's well-known style as in no way to suggest the painter. Another canvas of equal interest is an early Winslow Homer, "Defiance," which depicts a scene witnessed by Mr. Homer himself during the Civil War. A soldier stands on the ramparts, in an act of bravery or bravado, silhouetted against the sky, his comrades in the immediate foreground and the enemy in the distance. This canvas, too, is more finished than the majority of Homer's paintings. But despite this fact the artist has not painted out one jot or tittle of its strength. The picture is little less than a prize.

A long canvas by C. Harry Eaton, "Wet Day in October," showing a muddy road leading direct from the spectator to a clump of woods, is another favorite of the collector. In the middle foreground a farmer's horse is toiling over the heavy road. The draftsmanship is excellent, the color scheme is rich, and the atmosphere seems suffused with moisture from the reeking ground. The pictures by Murphy are all good and thoroughly characteristic of this

DEFIANCE
By Winslow Homer

artist's peculiar poetic treatment. His "An Early Fall" is perhaps the best.

Of a collection as extensive and varied as that of Mr. Gibbs, only a hint can be given of its manifold excellence. It would be foreign to the purpose of this article to give a list of the paintings and equally impossible to give descriptive details. The mention of a few names must suffice, and it will be noticed that Mr. Gibbs's predilection toward American work has not led him to be an indiscriminate buyer. Bruce Crane, Arthur Parton, David Johnson are all well represented, as are also Jervis McEntee, T. B. Craig, Charles H. Miller, C. Y. Turner, and Bliss Baker. J. J. Brown and Louis Moeller stand for the figure pictures that tell a story, and as a critic has said, there is humor and human nature in all the works by these artists in the collection. The gallery has a number of excellent war scenes by

C. X. Harris, Gilbert Gaul, Grolleron, and Berne-Bellecour. There are dainty figure pieces by W. M. Chase and J. G. Brown. Of the

THE NEST
By T. W. Wood

portraits, one of the most interesting is a dainty little picture of an old lady, by Ludwig Knaus, painted in grays and browns, and charming in its exemplification of an old-fashioned belle of a generation or two

EARLY FALL
By J. Francis Murphy

ago. Seifert's "Innocence" is a head equally charming because of its rich outlines and its wealth of color.

Dolph, Asti, and Wiles; Ronner, Robie, and Desgoffe; Birney, De Haas, and F. C. Jones; Warren Sheppard, Carleton Wiggins, and R. A. Blakelock; Percy Moran, Carle Blenner, William Morgan, and the two Harts, William and James M., and many another artist who has won for himself name and fame in his profession are represented in landscape, seascape, portraits, still life, and *genre* subjects. A few of the pictures, possibly, Mr. Gibbs might well spare from his collection, but for the most part the canvases are well selected and would be a credit to any private or public gallery in the country.

Of late years Mr. Gibbs has devoted much attention to the work of R. A. Blakelock, whose melancholy career was cut short a few years ago by mental collapse at a time when his wonderful power as a colorist and as an interpreter of nature was overcoming for him the prejudice excited by his early eccentricities. His canvases run the range from quiet and poetic pastorals to brilliant sunsets and impressive moonlight scenes, and in most of his works one detects the prevailing minor chord that was characteristic of the artist's life.

Mr. Gibbs has purchased fifty-eight of this artist's canvases, which reveal him in all his moods and in the full range of his powers. Some of these canvases are wild adventures into the realm of tonality, others are sane compositions painted with an absolute fidelity to nature, and all are interesting not less from the ability they display than from personal association. This collection of Blakelocks is perhaps the strongest evidence afforded by Mr. Gibbs's gallery of the marked evolution of the collector's tastes, and the fifty-eight canvases if put on exhibition—and this will likely be done this fall—would make little less than an event in American art.

In conclusion, a word about Mr. Gibbs may be acceptable to the reader. Essentially a man of affairs, with wide business interests and engrossing duties, the collection of pictures has been for him a pleasing pastime. Assemblyman, state senator, Republican candidate for mayor of New York, and Republican national committeeman from

WAITING
By Seymour J. Guy

the state of New York, he has for many years been one of the most active and influential statesmen and politicians in the country.

He was born at Seneca Falls, New York, March 22, 1845. He served with distinction throughout the Civil War, and on being mustered out managed various business interests until the formation of the Metropolitan Water Company of New York, of which corporation he has been managing director ever since. His controlling policy in the collection of pictures is but part and parcel of his business life, since in all his interests he is intensely American. As regards his art collection, he is unassuming and even retiring, and probably no American collector has been less actuated in his purchases by the spirit of speculation. His acquisition of fine paintings has been a natural outgrowth of his love of the beautiful and not a matter of barter and sale, and in the cases in which he has disposed of pictures his sales have invariably been for the purpose of improving his collection and not for the purpose of realizing on an investment.

It would be well for American art if there were more collectors like Mr. Gibbs, loyal to native-born artists, prone to see the excellence of home products, and willing to give painters on this side of the Atlantic the mead of patronage which is their due.

KIRK D. HENRY.

A RAINY DAY OFF STAR ISLAND
By M. F. H. De Haas

TEN POUND ISLAND
By Charles Abel Corwin
At Pan-American Exposition

PAINTINGS AT THE PAN-AMERICAN

The fine arts exhibition at the Pan-American may safely be termed one of its distinctive triumphs. When this has been said, however, the statement needs qualifying. Being primarily a loan exhibition, the works displayed lack the charm of novelty. There are few canvases shown that are new to those well-informed in art matters. Most of the pictures made their debut long since in some one or other of the principal American exhibitions, or have long hung in the galleries of public institutions. The freshest, though not the most interesting or important, canvases are those contributed by Canada and the other Pan-American countries outside the United States.

These words are not to be taken as an expression of criticism. It is inherent in the very nature of the exposition—and it is perhaps to be considered as one of its supreme merits—that its fine arts display should consist largely of salon works, prize-winners; in short, works that have been subjected to the criticism of juries and have held their own.

It was the avowed purpose of the projectors of the enterprise to gather together representative specimens of the work of American painters, sculptors, architects, and engravers. A conscientious effort was made to secure from artists, private purchasers, and public institutions an extensive collection of the finest productions of American origin possible. The display consists of about eight hundred exhibits, and as William A. Coffin, director of fine arts, says with pardonable pride, it is hard to find a noted artist who is not represented at all, and still harder to find one who is not represented by his best work.

The Albright gallery offers an almost ideal exhibition place. The pleasing green walls of its various rooms form a restful background for the brilliant display of paintings, and much credit is due to the hanging committee for the artistic arrangement of the exhibits. Due regard has been had to harmony of color schemes and subjects, and

CONNECTICUT HILLSIDE
By C. H. Hayden
At Pan-American Exposition

care has been taken not to "sky" pictures whose character and quality demand comparatively close inspection. The exhibition affords a most saisfactory presentation of Pan-American art, and taken all in all, it is to be doubted if the display could be much improved.

Naturally the exhibition does not lend itself to critical discussion—the exhibits for the most part have received due notice in former years. The present article, therefore, aims to give only a general idea of the exhibitors and a suggestion of the wealth of art that has been provided for the visitors to the exposition. The paintings have been arranged and catalogued by rooms, and a cursory survey of the different galleries will perhaps best give this general information.

The display begins in the vestibule, where the visitor finds ten or a dozen fine canvases, among which are Blashfield's "The Angel with the Flaming Sword," Robert Reid's "Moonrise," Charles H. Davis's "Summer Clouds," and Samuel Isham's "The Apple of Discord." The first gallery to the right presents, with a certain measure of propriety, the works of American artists residing abroad, though for

EVENING IN PICARDY
By Louis Paul Dessar
At Pan-American Exposition

the sake of graceful symmetry of grouping the pictures of other American artists are liberally interspersed.

Among the artists represented in this room are Frank D Millet with a group of five, and Edwin A. Abbey with his well-known picture, "The Penance of Eleanor, Duchess of Gloucester." Opposite these hang six characteristic portraits by John S. Sargent, all more or less familiar, and grouped with them are a number of charming landscapes by W. L. Lathrop. Close by Mr. Abbey's conspicuous canvas hang J. J. Shannon's "Miss Kitty," which won the first prize at the Carnegie Institute a year ago, and the same artist's picture of

THE END OF THE DAY
By Sergeant Kendall
At Pan-American Exposition

Mrs. Shannon, together with the famous portrait of Gladstone by John McLure Hamilton.

In the next room hangs a group of four works by Alexander Harrison, including his celebrated "Le Crépuscule," now the property of the St. Louis Art Museum. The center panel of this room is occupied by a group of five oils and two water-colors by James McNeill Whistler, representing him in the various styles of work for which he is celebrated. Above his group hang a landscape by Charles Caryl Coleman and a decorative work by Kenyon Cox, entitled "Poetry and Art." Other notable canvases in this room are by Howard Russell Butler, Walter Shirlaw, Edith Mitchell Prellwitz, Henry Prellwitz, Dana Marsh, and Robert Henri. John W. Alexander is represented by a group of three large pictures, the central one being his "Autumn."

Henry O. Tanner's "Daniel in the Lion's Den" forms the center of a group of rich-toned works on the left, prominent among which are two portraits by Edward Dufner, a Buffalo artist now resident in Paris. Two canvases by Augustus B. Koopman, here displayed, show that artist at his best. Another young artist residing in Paris, S. Seymour Thomas, exhibits his "After the Bath." Hanging over a group by Bridgman is a large picture, entitled "The Temple of the Winds," by Louis Loeb, full of rich color and decorative in form.

The center of another panel is occupied by a dainty piece by William T. Dannat, while hanging above it is a large work by W. L. Metcalf, depicting a scene in an Algerian market-place. In a corner of the room hangs a group of outdoor studies of female figures among flowers, by J. L. Stewart. The end of the room is filled by a large work by Charles Sprague Pearce, showing a characteristic French peasant with a flock of sheep.

Near by hang two exhibition pictures by Gari Melchers, and adjoining them a strong work by J. S. Risbing, and a canvas, entitled "Loading the Caravan," by E. L. Weeks, a particularly fine example of this artist's Eastern subjects. Julian Story shows a group of three pictures, including two portraits of his wife.

The center of the large gallery is occupied by a composition by Walter Gay, "French Breton Peasants at Prayer," which is subdued in color and pleasing. A group of three pictures at the right shows the work of Eugene Vail, while Walter MacEwen is represented by one large painting, the theme being a Puritan maiden who is charged with witchcraft. "Light Nights in Norway," by John Humphreys Johnson, shows that artist at his best. The subject is simple but strong, and full of delicate color.

In the corner of the gallery occupied by John Humphreys Johnson's group of three hangs also the well-known picture "Atala," by Lucius Hitchcock.

In one of the smaller side galleries is a medley of figure subjects, with landscapes and marines well interspersed. Prominent among the figure works is "The Son of Mary," by Elliott Daingerfield, and "The End of the Day," by Sergeant Kendall. Two notable landscapes in this room are by Charles Warren Eaton. A meadow scene, with sheep returning to the fold, is by Carleton Wiggins. Two brilliant marines by Charles H. Woodbury, and three pictures by Louis Paul Dessar, Daniel Huntington's portrait of Bishop Coxe, and the portrait of Thomas G. Platt, by Thomas W.

PORTRAIT OF THE REV. JAMES REED, OF BOSTON
By H. D. Murphy
At Pan-American Exposition

Wood, are also in this room. Other men represented are F. K. M. Rehn, R. M. Shurtleff, Frank Duveneck, Hugh H. Breckenridge, William H. Howe, E. L. Henry, James D. Smillie, and Thomas Eakens.

In the second small room is displayed a group of pictures by Albert Lynch, the representative of Peru at the Pan-American Exposition. Here also are the exhibits of the South American artists, three landscapes by William A. Coffin, director of fine arts, and canvases by Charles C. Curran and Henry B. Snell, his assistants. On the opposite wall hangs a group by the veteran J. G. Brown, showing four of his characteristic pictures, and near by is "The Hum of Mighty Workings," by Karl Hirschberg. Four moonlight landscapes represent the work of Charles Melville Dewey.

The original for the much admired poster, "Spirit of Niagara," by Mrs. Charles Cary, hangs in this room also. Near it are three interesting portraits by Lars G. Sellstedt. Two fine landscapes, hung one over the other, are by Leonard Ochtman, and beside them is Gilbert Gall's dramatic work, "Charge of the Battery." Two strong portraits of men in this room are by Thomas Eakens, of Philadelphia.

THE SKATERS
By Gari Melchers
At Pan-American Exposition

Crossing the sculpture court and entering one of the small galleries on the west side of the building, one finds strong portraits by Eastman Johnson, William H. Hyde, August Franzen, William Thorne, and Benjamin C. Porter; landscapes by Ben Foster, William Sartain, Edward F. Rook, W. Elmer Schofield, Worthington Whittredge, Charles A. Platt, W. L. Metcalf, and Arthur Parton; marines by Howard Russell Butler and F. K. M. Rehn; cattle pictures with figures by Lyell Carr and C. Morgan McIlhenney; ideal decorative works

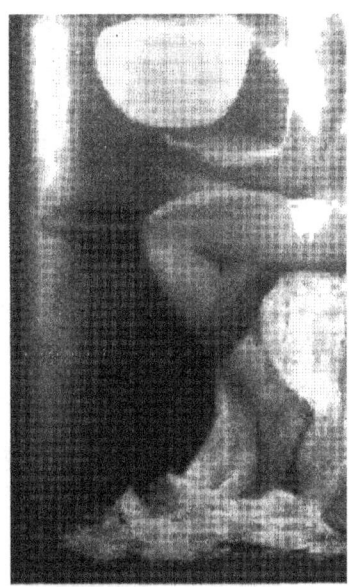

LANTERN GLOW, PASTEL
By Hugh H. Breckenridge
At Pan-American Exposition

by Will H. Low, Kenyon Cox, and Louise Cox. Henry Golden Dearth and J. H. Twachtman have fine groups of landscapes with one figure picture in each.

A small room offers a choice display of water-colors, the most prominent being a group of twenty-one subjects painted in the Bahamas and Bermuda Islands by Winslow Homer. These works are most characteristic of the rugged strength of that distinguished artist. To the right of this group are wintry landscapes by Leonard Ochtman and Walter L. Palmer. The latter artist is also represented by other pictures, among them being two views in Venice. Hanging opposite are water-colors by Horatio Walker, Harvey Ellis, Joseph Lindon Smith, E. L. Blumenschein, Arthur J. Keller, and other well-known artists. Opposite the group by Winslow Homer is a fine panel with works by Ross Turner, Mrs. Rosina E. Sherwood, George Wharton Edwards, Mrs. E. M. Scott, Albert E. Sterner, Mrs. Sarah C. Sears, R. M. Shurtleff, C. Morgan McIlhenney, and Arthur J. Keller. On the right and left panels are works by Louis Loeb, Alexander Schilling, A. Phimister Proctor, William J. Whittemore, Carlton T. Chapman, Maurice Prendergast, and B. West Clinedinst.

In the small gallery to the right of the water-color room is the exhibit by the artists of Canada, arranged by the Royal Canadian Academy, of which more will be said on another occasion. From the Canadian room the visitor enters the large west gallery, replete with the best work of the artists resident in America. In the center of the largest panel hangs a group composed of landscapes by Dwight W. Tryon and figures by Thomas W. Dewing. Over this group hangs a water-color, entitled "Gloria," by Albert Herter, a fit companion to the striking work of Tryon and Dewing. In the center of the north room is a group by Horatio Walker, and over this hangs an immense canvas by Thomas Moran, the painter of America's great Western scenery. To the right is a group of portraits by William M. Chase, showing vigorous brush work and sureness of touch, and to the left two figures by Abbott H. Thayer and one by George De Forest Brush.

Near by are Cox's "Harp Player," one of his finest works; "Carnations," by Maria Oakley Dewing, full of delicacy and subtile charm; three landscapes by J. Francis Murphy in his best style; Frederic P. Vinton's fine portrait of Thomas G. Appleton; Robert Brandagee's "The Portrait of an Artist"; splendid river views by E. W. Redfield; and three portraits, rich in coloring and full of character, by Robert W. Vonnoh.

In one corner of this room hangs "Dorothea and Francesca," one of Cecilia Beaux's most successful portraits; charming figure pictures by Douglas Volk; and winter twilight landscapes, by Charles Morris Young. In another corner are canvases in characteristic manner by Robert Reid, Frank W. Benson, and Childe Hassam, together with paintings by J. Alden Weir, including landscapes, ideal and figure subjects, and portraits. In an adjoining panel are portraits by Irving R. Wiles, a charming figure in green by W. Howard Hart, and three of Bruce Crane's best landscapes, including two prize works.

DANIEL IN THE LION'S DEN
By H. O. Tanner
At Pan-American Exposition

Entering the gallery in the southwest corner of the building, one finds a large group of figure subjects, the Samuel T. Shaw prize fund pictures of the last ten years—a notable set, comprising works of Robinson, Tarbell, Benson, H. O. Walker, Chase, Barse, and Wiles.

To the right are portraits by Wilton Lockwood, Charles Hopkinson, Cecilia Beaux, Frank Fowler, Andreas Anderson, J. Carroll Beckwith, Anna Lea Merritt, and Emily Sartain, together with two little landscapes by Charles H. Davis and Ryder's "The Temple of the Winds." Near by is a group of pictures representing H. Siddons Mowbray, some brilliant, others somber in color. In another panel are landscapes and marines, by F. W. Kost, Walter Clark, Theodore Robinson, George H. Bogert, the late Robert Eichelberger, and other artists. Other pleasing canvases are by Francis C. Jones and William T. Smedley.

In the last large gallery are hung many of the works by deceased painters, the principal group being by George Inness, showing seven of his best canvases. There are splendid examples by Wyant, including two now publicly exhibited for the first time, and lent by the artist's widow. Near these are "Westchester Hills" and "Normandy Farm," by Homer Martin; "Moonlight," by R. E. Blakelock; "Chloe and Sam," by the late Thomas Hodengen, and "Solitude," by William Bliss Baker.

Among the works by living painters in this room are "Siegfried" and "Jonah," by A. P. Rider; "Sea and Rain," by George H. Bogert; a group of four fine landscapes by H. W. Ranger; "Christ and Nicodemus" and a figure study, "Autumn," by John La Farge; a "Sunset" and a "Moonlight," by Robert C. Meyer; characteristic works by George Inness, Jr.; two good examples by William Keith; "La Cigale," by Wyatt Eaton; a group of landscapes by R. Swain Gifford, and several by Charles Rollo Peters; and C. Y. Turner's "The Days that are No More."

HERBERT S. GRANVILLE.

THE SOUL BETWEEN DOUBT AND FAITH
By Elihu Vedder
Copyright by Elihu Vedder, and by Curtis & Cameron, Boston

BRUSH AND PENCIL

Vol. VIII   AUGUST, 1901   No. 5

REVIVAL OF INTEREST IN ETCHING

It is scarcely twenty years since etching, "the art of Rembrandt," as it has been called, had literally a new birth in America. For a time plates of the highest order were produced by a number of gifted American artists, and it seemed that the art was destined to have a more glorious future in this country than in the Old World.

REMBRANDT APPUYE, 1639
By Rembrandt

Farrer, Falconer, the Morans, James D. Smillie, R. Swain Gifford, F. S. Church, Bellows, Parrish, Frank Duveneck, Chase, Miller, Van Elten, Coleman, Otto H. Bacher, Blum, Vanderhoff, Whistler, and scores of other artists gained high repute with the needle, and centered upon themselves the attention of that element of the public who delight in dainty bits of nature exquisitely rendered in the soft, velvet lines which the copper-plate alone can produce. Of this chosen coterie of pioneers who made such a brilliant start in the early eighties, practically the only man who retains his deep interest in etching to-day is James D. Smillie.

The art of etching has been denominated a fad, and has been declared moribund, if not dead. The brief but promising period during which it thrived in America has been likened to the life of most fads, that have their brief day of popularity and then sink into oblivion. The fact is, however, that etching was not, is not a fad.

THE TOWING PATH
By Seymour Haden

It is an art of a high order, one that appeals and will ever appeal to cultured tastes, that lapsed from popularity through the force of circumstances which many of those most deeply interested in it foresaw.

It were a pity if an art honored by such men as Rembrandt, Van Dyck, Jacque, Flameng, Millet, Meryon, Lalanne, Fortuny, Corot, Meissonier, Rajon, Buhot, Detaille, Haden, and the Americans already named should be forced into retirement, and there are now indications of a revival of interest that may restore the needle to its former prestige.

The two things primarily responsible for the decline of etching are commercialism and the dvelopment of reproductive processes. Frederick Keppel, a connoisseur and a shrewd business man, predicted years ago the fate that would overtake the copper-plate.

"What are the future prospects of etching considered as a fine art?" he asked. And he answered: "The winter of obscurity and neglect is over, and the glorious summer of prosperity has come; but herein lies a real danger. With popularity its true artistic side may be ignored; quantity may be considered rather than quality; the art may be boomed and exploited for sordid commercial ends; and men who are incapable of it as an art may ply the making of etchings as a trade."

That is just what happened. Invention has made a travesty of first, second, and third states,

THE PALACE OF WESTMINSTER
By Felix Buhot

remarque proofs, and everything else that collectors of prints prize.

When etchings were at the height of their popularity, cleverness set itself to work to devise a means whereby the limited possibilities of a plate could be almost indefinitely multiplied, and etchings could be run off for a few cents apiece, about

THE THAMES EMBANKMENT
By Joseph Pennell

as we now run off newspapers. A short time and the market was glutted.

An etched copper-plate, as is well-known, is very susceptible to wear, and at the outside, a few hundred perfect impressions is all it will yield. By hardening and coating processes it was found possible to make a plate yield thousands of prints where formerly it yielded only hundreds, or even tens. Cleverness went further, and supplied the remarque to the paper, and even the artist's signature, before ever the etching was printed upon it.

It was the mere commercial expedient of supplying to the public "something as good as the genuine" for a mere song. This virtually sounded the death-knell of etching. Artists with more industry than ability were brought into requisition. The quality of

LE CANAL ST. MARTIN
By Maxime Lalanne

A WATER MEADOW
By Seymour Haden

work deteriorated with the multiplication of prints and the cheapening of price. The various states easily discernible in the best days of etching soon lost their value.

The thousandth impression under the new régime of the commercial etchers was as clear and distinct as the first impression, and was quite as likely to be sold as such. It is not at all surprising, therefore, that the public should have grown wary in its acceptance of protestations, and should have regarded the "genuine first state etchings" offered for sale about as we of to-day are wont to regard the "absolutely faithful three-color reproductions" of paintings given free as supplements with the Sunday papers.

This stage having been reached, the majority of the artists who formerly had done such creditable work naturally sought a new medium of artis-

ANNIE SEATED
By J. M. Whistler

tic expression. James D. Smillie, however, has remained loyal to his first love. He is convinced that etching, degraded as it has been by commercial enterprise, has yet a great future as a high art. In a recent public announcement he said:

"Etching at its best is a noble art, and so long as appreciation for the work of the masters remains it cannot die and be given over to the collector of curiosities of the past. The art can exist at its best only where there are talent and enthusiasm, independent of desire for gain on the part of the etcher, and an educated appreciation on the part of a select public."

PORTRAIT OF MEISSONIER
By Paul Rajon

With the conviction set forth in this announcement, Mr. Smillie has set himself to work to develop, so far as he can, the conditions necessary ultimately to put etching on its old basis. A fortuitous circumstance has favored his enterprise. A sister of the late A. H. Baldwin, an artist of much cleverness with the needle, sought some four years ago to perpetuate the memory of her brother by creating an endowment to be known as the A. H. Baldwin fund, the revenue

AN OLD OAK
By Charles Storm van's Gravesande

of which was to be devoted to promoting interest in etching and to encouraging students to do work worthy of the art. The income of the fund has wisely been intrusted to Mr. Smillie, and it is to the credit of the donor that she made such a wise choice of an administrator of her gift.

Mr. Smillie's field of operation naturally is in the schools of the National Academy of Design, where, without recompense, he has devoted himself arduously to the instruction of a class in etching. The Baldwin fund now furnishes two prizes, which are given each year to the two students producing the first and second best plates, the remainder of the revenue of the fund being devoted to the purchase of fine etching proofs, partly for class purposes, and partly to form the nucleus of what it is hoped will in time become a magnificent collection of etchings.

PORTRAIT OF THE SCULPTOR DALOU
By Alphonse Legros

Already a considerable number of the choicest of prints has been secured. The fact that the purchases have been made under the direct supervision of Mr. Smillie vouches for the quality of the collection.

A word as to the methods followed in the class may be acceptable to the reader. A studio fitted out with a full equipment for etching and copper-plate printing has been funished by the Academy from the fund provided by the donor. Etching is an art that requires peculiar aptitude on the part of the student It is a case of many being called but few being chosen. The would-be etchers who apply for admission to the class are for the most part students who have won the rank of honor-men in the advanced academy school, but these are carefully sifted out, and those who do not manifest the sympathetic temperament necessary for the execution of high-class work are discouraged by the teacher, who is not slow to inform them

ABSIDE DE NOTRE-DAME DE PARIS
By Charles Meryon

INLAND PORT
By Charles A. Platt

LA PARTIE PERDUE
By Louis Ruet

that they have not chosen the right medium for their artistic expression.

There is doubtless ample field for reproductive etchers, as, for instance, witness the work of Leopold Flameng, Paul Rajon, and many another celebrated etcher. But the charm of the art lies largely in original work, and for this reason Mr. Smillie wisely seeks to develop painter-etchers rather than reproductive etchers. The class at the Academy works directly from life models. Ban is put on the very thought of commercialism, and the students are told, as the gospel of the revived art, that they are to put from their minds all thought of making the needle a source of pecuniary gain. They are encouraged to work freely, and spontaneously and to seek their only reward in love of the art itself.

Thus far the efforts of Mr. Smillie have been signally successful. He has succeeded in arousing a certain enthusiasm among the students that has been of material assistance in his work. It is his ambition not merely to impart proper instruction to those fortunate enough to be admitted to the class and to build up a fine print department in the institution, but to make the class nothing less than the basis of a

THE TANGLED SKEIN
By Gaston Rodrigues

movement which will perpetuate and extend itself. For this purpose those students who show the most aptitude for the work and develop the greatest facility in it are offered positions as assistant instructors, and Mr. Smillie expresses the belief that he will in this way succeed not only in making etching a permannt feature in the Academy's work, but in sending forth to other centers of art education well-equipped men who will strive, as he is striving, to popularize and elevate the old art. Care is taken to make these prospective teachers as many-sided as possible, and for this reason the instruction given covers simple line, dry-point, soft ground, aquatint, and mezzotint.

THE ELMS OF CENON
By Maxime Lalanne

It is not to be supposed from what has been said that Mr. Smillie has smooth sailing or an easy time in his enterprise. It is the exceptional student who is so circumstanced that he can afford to devote a protracted period of time to the development of an art merely for the love of it. The necessities of life are uncompromising, and most students in mapping out their course have before them the development of the means of support, or at least a reasonable source of revenue. It follows, therefore, that the perpetuation of Mr. Smillie's movement—and it may be said that his is the only class in America in which specific and comprehensive instruction in etching is given—depends upon the discovery of a sufficient body of enthusiasts like himself, men willing to do their best and trust to a refining taste to make their work appreciated.

It is a significant fact that the right class of work does sell. The prints of many an etcher of repute a generation ago can now scarcely be had at the art stores, having been banished through lack of demand on the part of the public. But Whistlers and Hadens always sell, and it is a question whether in the army of students now at our art schools there are not scores of unpracticed Whistlers and Hadens whose work would be avidiously sought by the public. One can but wish Mr. Smillie success in his efforts to discover these untrained geniuses and direct their energies on proper lines.

Seymour Haden has been termed the "prince of modern etchers," but Whistler is his close second. It is to be doubted if the English

PREMIERE LECON D'EQUITATION
By Charles Jacque

surgeon, whose name is so familiar in art circles, ever gave more pregnant advice on the art that made him famous than did the eccentric American in his famous propositions. Had etchers adhered to the letter of Whistler's dicta, probably even commercialism and modern processes would not have resulted so disastrously as they have to etching as a high art.

With the prospect of revived interest in the copper-plate and needle, it is worth while here to quote the eleven propositions that Whistler observed in his own work and advised others to observe in theirs. He maintained:

1. That in art, it is criminal to go beyond the means used in its exercise.

2. That the space to be covered should always be in proper relation to the means used for covering it.

3. That in etching, the means used, or the instrument employed,

being the finest possible point, the space to be covered should be small in proportion.

4. That all attempts to overstep the limits insisted upon by such proportions are thoroughly inartistic, and tend to reveal the paucity of the means used, instead of concealing the same, as required by art in its refinement.

5. That the huge plate, therefore, is an offense; its undertaking an unbecoming display of determination and ignorance; its accomplishment a triumph of unthinking earnestness and uncontrollable energy—endowments of the "duffer."

6. That the custom of "remarque" emanates from the amateur, and reflects his foolish facility beyond the border of his picture, thus testifying to his unscientific sense of its dignity.

NELSON MONUMENT, TRAFALGAR SQUARE
By Joseph Pennell

7. That it is odious.

8. That, indeed, there should be no margin on the proof to receive such "remarque."

9. That the habit of margin, again, dates from the outsider, and continues with the collector in his unreasoning connoisseurship—taking curious

EAGLE WHARF
By J. M. Whistler

PAYSAN RENTRANT DU FUMIER
By J. F. Millet

pleasure in the quantity of paper.

10. That the picture ending where the frame begins, and in the case of the etching the white mount being inevitably, because of its color, the frame, the picture thus extends itself irrelevantly through the margin to the mount.

11. That wit of this kind would leave six inches of raw canvas between the painting and its gold frame, to delight the purchaser with the quality of the cloth.

There is a certain sarcasm and grim humor about these statements, but couched in the Whistleresque diction is the soundest of sound advice. It *is* criminal in art to go beyond the means used in its exercise; the space to be covered *should* be in proper relation to the means used; the huge plate *is* an offense; the remarque *is* foolish embellishment; and so on throughout the whole list of Whistler's "thats."

The men who gave rebirth to the old art in the early eighties worked on legitimate lines and were not offenders against Whistler's dicta. They respected their means of artistic expression and recognized the limitations

SHEPHERD AND FLOCK
By Leopold Lesigne

placed upon the needle. For the most part they gauged the size of their plates by the point with which they had to cover them, and were content to turn out an artistic trifle, suggestive in its lines and beautiful in its finish, rather than a wall-covering print in the commercial estimate of which area was a more important factor than fineness of execution or correctness of interpretation.

Mr. Smillie has never been guilty of producing commercial monstrosities, and the regeneration of the old art, the revival of the moribund fad, if you please, may safely be left to his tact and good judgment.

An odd shifting of taste has given a certain popularity to colored

A LIONESS AND CUBS
By Evert Van Muyden

etching, but one can scarcely regard this variation in product as other than an excrescence on legitimate work. If the art revives, as indications seem to point, lovers of the beautiful in America will doubtless prefer a masterful expression in black-and-white of simple and picturesque scenes to hybrid products tricked out with touches of color that seem foreign to the very nature of legitimate etching.

It is only natural that the lapse of time should bring new ideas and new tastes—it would be strange did not the years beget new forms or variations of art. But there is a rare beauty in etching as Rembrandt and his followers practiced it, a beauty that needs no tricks or trimmings to recommend it to cultured people. The charm of the copper-plate is not recondite or mysterious: it is simple, direct. It is the charm of suggestive outline, of smooth-cut or minutely irregular strokes, of velvety effects of ink on suitable paper; of delicate, refined, or bold treatment. That the possibilities of the needle have all been apprehended no one would venture to contend. On the contrary, most experts maintain that the highest development of the art is to be reached in perfecting old methods rather than in inventing the novelties of an hour. If perchance some fledgling etcher of to-day or of the near future should eclipse all the old masters of the past in straight, legitimate work, the old masters need have no fear of losing prestige, any more than the old masters of painting who contributed to the development of their art. The Whistlers and Hadens have no cause to be jealous of mere innovators; they would not be jealous of men who could carry their art to higher perfection.

Morris T. Everett.

THE CONVALESCENT
By J. J. Tissot

THE CULT OF GRANDPAS IN ART

George Brandes, the Danish writer and the friend of all workers in the arts, recently said in an exchange:

"One can be an excellent book-keeper, chief of department, grocer, and the like at seventy. Also an honored contributor to scientific periodicals or an editor of established publications; there is no limit of age for clergymen—the more childlike he becomes the better he is suited for his profession. But with people who conceive and execute ideas, with creative genius, great artists, thinkers, poets, it is quite another matter. The creative powers of a man of thirty or forty years are vastly superior to those of a grandpa.

"There seems to be a law of nature that says that no man shall get recognition before his fiftieth or sixtieth year. No matter how 'great' he is, he must wait. Only when he has begun to get tired, when the fire is dying out, when hard life has blunted his originality and his love of the ideal—only then recognition comes.

"And it isn't necessarily his best work that caused the change in his fortunes. Those best works he created ten or twenty years before his rise in the world, but in the mean time he has polished off his edges, his ideas on persons and things are now more conventional, hence he becomes acceptable himself, and so it happens that not only his present works, but also his past offenses, are lauded to the skies. And though knowing that his powers are on the wane, he continues to produce, and the older he gets, the heartier public opinion applauds him. He may continue to send works into the world for thirty or forty years; he will always have people's attention, and no one dares attack him.

"Why is this so? First, because the public doesn't like any fomenting, heaven-storming geniuses. Racers are well, but most people are content with a cab-horse. And again, genius, when it has starved long enough, attains the glory of venerableness. 'This sculptor, this writer, this master of the brush—see his gray hair; he has worked hard; we must do something for him.'

"When the *vox populi* has spoken, don't touch the popular favorite. Why not? let me ask. Why shouldn't the young genius, he in whom all the glory of youth lives and strives, say to this belated idol, 'I have long admired thee for what thou didst do when thou wert as old as I, but thy present work is beneath criticism.'

"Young man, you needn't envy the older on account of the experience he possesses. Your youth is of more value in the battle of life than any amount of experience. Of course, there are young

STUDIO, WHERE GRANDPAS AND GRANDSONS WORK

old men and youth that is old. With such, years do not count. It is their personality that tips the balance-bar one way or the other.

"That old age masters our creative powers, that we cannot prevent; it's in the order of things. But that discrowned genius approves of it, that its measure of honor and esteem grows all the time, like hair—that is man's work, and there is, besides the comical aspect, a certain amount of danger in it. Everybody admits that the young create really powerful works. Why must they wait until they are old and decrepit? The system is fundamentally wrong, but the 'old master' won't admit it, and the young haven't authority enough to assert themselves and change things about. Hence we shall continue the cult of grandpas, at the cost of youth. But, let me repeat, it's against the order of nature. Nature has endowed youth with creative power, and youth does create."

RECENT WORK OF ILLUSTRATORS—
M. H. SQUIRE AND E. MARS

Much clever work is now being done by women illustrators. The following plates are fairly characteristic of the drawings of Miss M. H. Squire and Miss E. Mars, who have collaborated in the illumination of several books.

WHERE GO THE BOATS?
By Miss M. H. Squire and Miss E. Mars
From "A Child's Garden of Verse," by Robert Louis Stevenson. R. H. Russell, Publisher
Copyright, 1900, by Robert Howard Russell

PICTURE BOOKS IN WINTER
By Miss M. H. Squire and Miss E. Mars
From "A Child's Garden of Verse," by Robert Louis Stevenson. R. H. Russell, Publisher
Copyright, 1900, by Robert Howard Russell

SHADOW MARCH
By Miss M. H. Squire and Miss E. Mars
From "A Child's Garden of Verse," by Robert Louis Stevenson. R. H. Russell, Publisher
Copyright, 1900, by Robert Howard Russell

THE LITTLE LAND
By Miss M. H. Squire and Miss E. Mars
From " A Child's Garden of Verse," by Robert Louis Stevenson. R. H. Russell, Publisher
Copyright, 1900, by Robert Howard Russell

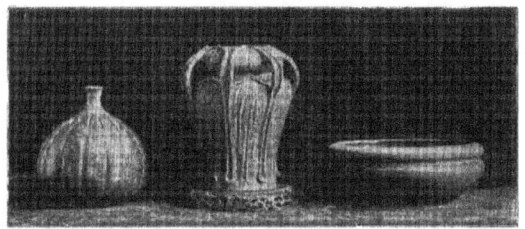

GRUEBY POTTERY
Designed by Geo. P. Kendrick
Illustrating Simplicity of Design

NEW DEPARTURE IN STUDY OF ARCHITECTURAL DESIGN

Heresies usually make interesting chapters of history, and the heresies of art are no exception to the rule. It is the general custom, hallowed by centuries of practice, to require of the student of architectural design a long and tedious course of copying classical masterpieces. The theory underlying this method of instruction is identical with that which impelled Sir Joshua Reynolds and many another of the great teachers of pictorial art to be such ardent advocates of the study of the "masters"—to give the students the benefit of former achievements and to ground them on the principles and types that have met the critics' approval. He, therefore, who would advocate the breaking away from time-honored usage can be termed little less than a heretic. In such guise appears Emil Lorch of the Art Institute of Chicago.

That the prevailing system of education has its advantages, none will deny, but that it has its evils many contend. It certainly discloses to the student the wealth of former attainments, and starts him on his career from the vantage-ground of centuries of experience. On the other hand, it is maintained that the practice has grafted on the new world a host of old-world ideas, has made our architecture a hybrid mixture of styles foreign to the spirit of the people,

JAPANESE STENCIL
Design for Study

CLASSICAL GREEK STUDIES
Illustrating Conventional Methods

and has tended to retard and impair strong national development. In view of this, it has been urged that less devotion should be accorded to the past, and more attention should be paid to developing the student's own inventive ability.

Mr. Lorch is a firm believer in the system of art education arranged and directed by Arthur W. Dow, who contends that space-art may be called "visual music," and may be criticised and studied from this point of view, and whose system has for its central thought the expression of beauty rather than mere representation. Mr. Dow, therefore, drills his pupils from the outset in simple, harmonious arrangements, keeps the possibilities of their minds freshly before them, teaches them to avoid the conventional and commonplace,' and shows them that "poverty of ideas is no characteristic of the artist, and that no work is of value unless it expresses the personality of the creator." In a word, he seeks to discourage the copyist and encourage the creator, making the student resourceful, self-reliant, and original, rather than a manipulator of foreign ideals and models.

To carry this new system into the field of architectural design, and make it contribute toward the development of a strongly individualistic and indigenous architecture, is something of an innovation, and the following suggestions are well worthy of consideration. ED.

Creative ability and beauty and fitness of expression distinguish the artist from the mere workman or laborer; in architecture it is this power, that of finding an artistic solution of an otherwise purely utilitarian problem, which distinguishes that greatest art craftsman, the architect, from the builder. And this full creative power comes, as a rule, only with the matured individual, who, arrived at a stage where, having developed himself and mastered the technical side of his art, is able grandly to amalgamate all the elements of his problem into one powerful result or expression.

In architectural design instruction—how to strengthen and draw out the analytical power, the appreciation and invention of the architectural student, to healthfully develop his imagination, train him to represent his ideas clearly in order that he may convey them to others for execution, teach him the terms or materials of his own art and the fundamental principles of all art—and thus give him means for individual artistic growth—how best to prepare this student that he may build beautifully as well as soundly, finding for each problem a personal and appropriate solution, or in other words, how to make him *not* an *adaptive* but a *creative* worker, or an artist-builder, an architect—is not, or should not, this be the highest and ideal end of architectural design study?

My belief is, that this end can be most nearly attained by exercises in pure design, from the very beginning of the first year, followed by what is called applied or industrial design throughout the remainder

REPRODUCED FROM COLOR-PRINT
By Arthur W. Dow
Suggestion for Developing Invention

of the course, parallel with the regular architectural design study, and *in order to develop as much as possible the student's perceptive power, his appreciation of the beauty of line, form, and color, and the necessity of harmonious inter-relation between these to produce beauty,* leaving the study of historic forms to a later period in his course, studying the styles of art and architecture as illustrations of expression during various epochs and under certain conditions rather than as absolute standards for the designer of to-day; that if a student cannot find time to

COMPOSITION IN COLOR, FOUR TONES
By M. J. Littig
Simple Study Exercise

make an original design of a support or other architectural member serving a structural and decorative purpose, how can he be expected to solve pleasingly, intelligently, and with sympathy the larger and more intricate problems which involve considerations of location, light and shade, color of material, etc., and which will need a consistent treatment of the whole and its parts? Further, that it is easier to teach the student certain dominant, fundamental principles, by beginning with exercises with elements of one and two dimensions than of three, of which latter he has at first little or no conception, and that when the third dimension is employed, it should be in a way to enable the student to fully realize his problem on paper by also modeling it out in clay—my idea being that while at present we begin where others left off, instruction in architectural design should begin farther back and as simply and directly as possible.

SIMPLE EXERCISES IN DESIGN

Now, that sense which arranges, relates, and unites the elements of an architectural design is largely a decorative one. Be it the arrangement of the spots of color in a picture, the masses or the voids and solids of a building, or the grouping of several buildings, the arrangement of windows within elevations, of moldings about openings, or the panels of a door, the members of a cornice, the design of a mantelpiece, or of a chair or a vase, that sense *which directs an arrangement of elements at once pleasing and practical, and which idealizes a mere element of service and use into one of beauty*—this sense is largely a decorative one. All artists are continually seeking for harmonious and pleasing arrangement, organization, or composition.

THE DANDELION LAMP
By Louis C. Tiffany
Showing Harmony of Material and Design

The artist-artisan does on a small scale what the architect does on a more extended one, only he does it so very much better, one reason being that he can more easily and fully grasp his problem in all its bearings of use, material, and appearance, and thus can produce a consistent result. I have in mind a noted American worker in glass whose works may be found in many foreign museums, who developed a new beauty in this material, and having given it many novel and beautiful forms, wrought in it a decoration fully suited to the character of the material and the forms. Very few of our architects could do, or aim to do, this, having no time themselves and no helpers who have the ability so to study their designs.

That in the attainment of this end in the architectural training of to-day everywhere there is something wanting has been claimed by many; it is also maintained that one of the greatest faults lies in the drill in the Orders and in classic architecture. Up to the present time it cannot be said, however, that suggestions for strengthening the present methods of teaching design in the architectural schools have been of a very practical nature.

In such instruction the student's first lessons should undoubtedly be the most carefully thought out, as these will always either help or retard his development and largely determine the character of his future work.

In a paper read before the Chicago Architectural Club, March 4, 1901, I stated that, rather than be taught to memorize and use a series of highly idealized forms, or the Orders, and from them and their use learning principles of design, I believed he should at once, upon entering the architectural school, be given exercises which will develop and clearly illustrate the fundamental, universal principles of design—thus enabling him for himself to recognize their presence under different conditions in all great works and use them intelligently.

Having an appreciation of these principles, he himself could almost study the history of architecture and of ornament, and be depended upon for an intelligent use of historic forms when such forms are required.

Various new ideas that have appeared during the past few years, and which are now producing excellent results with children in grade schools and with professional art students in decorative and pictorial composition, would form the starting-point, as comparatively little knowledge of drawing is required. I refer to the excellent work being done by Messrs. Ross and Dow. It would be found, too, that with such work as a beginning, the student would willingly study free-hand drawing to train eye and hand, in order to attain facility in representing his ideas.

CLASSICAL GREEK STUDIES
Illustrating Conventional Methods

Exercises based upon such ideas would naturally be of the most simple kind, and would begin with something fully within the student's comprehension; he could thus from the very beginning be doing creative work, exercise his ingenuity, and become sensitive and alert to beauty in its simplest forms.

"FAVRILE" GLASS
By Louis C. Tiffany
Sample of Unconventional Design

The student would then begin by making simple decorative arrangements of straight and curved lines, then of lines and areas or spots of different values within given spaces, finally adding color. The next step would be to have these spots or spaces designed or originated by him and by conventionalizing well-known local flower or plant forms, preparing the way for ornament having national characteristics, as well as leading to a study of the beauty of nature. Then would follow the design of simple objects whose use, as well as the nature of the material to be employed, could be entirely understood by students, as in a piece of pottery, a stone seat, or a bookcase, and also thus the forms that may be possible in that material, for further illustration of the materials and processes, visiting places where such objects are made.

In some cases, as in a vase or a door-knocker, the design should be carried out on a small scale in clay for a *full sense of its form*, and through this sense of touch and consequent understanding of form it will later be possible, by making, on a small scale, clay models of some of his building problems, to bring the student to a real conceptive power of solid form combinations and appearances.

JAPANESE STENCIL
Design for Study

I believe such exercises could profitably be pursued during the first year, and continued after that parallel with the larger problems in planning and design. In this manner many of the elements of a

OIL LAMP, BY LOUIS C. TIFFANY
The Bowl and Shade of tiny bits of "Favrile" Glass put together
Example of Unique Invention

building could successively be taken up, and an intimate and necessary knowledge gained of the artistic possibilities of many of the materials employed in architectural construction.

Through pure and applied design, then, I believe the young student will most easily and most quickly develop an appreciation of composition or arrangement, and be better prepared for the study of architectural design.

Crude at first, such designs would soon grow in strength and significance, and the student, enjoying his personal mastery and solution of the problems, would work with ever-increasing love and interest—really launched in creative work, discovering that within each problem lies its solution, that proportion is not fixed but relative in its nature—lead him to a true understanding of established forms and a much greater respect for their use, and above all help him to *work with a fuller consciousness and realization of the completed or carried-out appearance of his design*, thus better preparing him for a mastery of his art.
EMIL LORCH.

CLASSICAL GREEK STUDY
Illustrating Conventional Methods

SCULPTURE AT THE PAN-AMERICAN

Sculpture is more conspicuously represented at the Pan-American Exposition than any other branch of the fine arts. Its name is literally redundancy. From entrance to exit, along esplanade, on buildings, in nooks and corners, one finds symbolic figures and allegorical groups in profusion. In comparison with this wealth of purely ornamental and structural sculpture, the exhibit of the more serious and enduring work in the galleries is comparatively feeble.

One might be inclined to criticise this excess of decorative statuary, were it not that much of it is carefully studied for the purpose it is meant to subserve, is festive in its suggestion, and pleasing in its general effect.

This adoption of sculpture for decorative purposes at the exposition is the culmination of a policy begun by the Columbian exposition at Chicago in 1893, and followed with marked success at the recent Paris exposition. As late as 1853, at the great English exposition, both buildings and grounds were devoid of sculptural embellishments. It is due to the projectors of the White City at Chicago, in 1893, that statuary came to the fore as an artistic feature, and the grand result obtained on that occasion is primarily responsible for its use at Paris. While opinions will likely

TOLERANCE
By Hermann Metzen

differ as to this masque of allegory at Buffalo, it is probable that Karl Bitter, director of sculpture at the exposition, planned wisely when he undertook to eclipse former efforts in the line of sculptural embellishment.

As might naturally be expected, one finds at Buffalo some of the best work in decorative sculpture that has yet been produced, and at the same time no inconsiderable number of pieces that lend themselves to adverse criticism. It is in the very nature of an enterprise of this sort, however, that there should be a wide range in the quality of the work produced—a uniformity of excellence would not fall within the scope of human possibilities.

One would scarcely find fault with the predominating note of the

BIRTH OF ATHENE
By Michel Tonetti

festive that characterizes so many of the groups, but one would wish to see less of self-obtrusive allegory, which for the most part is meaningless without a key. It was said in a recent issue of BRUSH AND PENCIL that the symbolic meaning of the color scheme of the exposition would never in itself suggest a hidden meaning to the casual observer, and that even after a full explanation the implied story of the colors would be accepted by the visitor more out of courtesy to the designer of the scheme than through conviction as to the forcefulness of the symbolism. In the same way it may now be said of the sculptural effects of the exposition that they are decorative, pleasing, but that there is an excess of sculpture whose allegorical meaning one has to take on trust, and in place of whose elaborate symbolism one would welcome something less pretentious.

Again, the statuary impresses one as being somewhat too obtrusive. It suggests the idea that it dominates instead of being subservient to the whole landscape and architectural scheme. Simplicity of effect is marred by numbers; vistas pleasing from a landscape standpoint are disturbed, if not destroyed, by

THE ARTS
By Charles A. Lopez

THE QUADRIGA
From the first sketch modeled by A. P. Proctor

groups suggestive of architectural motives. One has forced upon him the sense that the purely decorative sculpture of the great enterprise is overdone.

In defense of this it may be urged that the whole exposition is a temporary pageant, that its spirit is essentially festive, and that embellishing features which would be scarcely admitted into permanent buildings or permanent park improvements would be perfectly admissible into a sort of dream city invented to please or delight for an hour, and thenceforth to live only in recollection. This position is in a measure defensible.

PORTRAIT OF MRS. CHARLES GRAFLY
By Charles Grafly

The projectors of the Buffalo fair wished to differentiate it from all preceding enterprises of a similar nature. Certain conditions lent themselves readily to unique treatment, and the directors were not slow to avail themselves of the possibilities offered them. The proximity of Buffalo, for instance, to Niagara Falls gave unrivaled opportunities for electrical display, and the topographical features of the exposition site made possible an ornateness of treatment that would be scarcely permissible had conditions been other than they were—an ornateness of treatment in which color and the beauty of sculptured form would naturally take a leading part. The Pan-American Exposition has already won for itself the name of the Rainbow City. It might as appropriately win for itself the name of the Electric City or the City of Sculpture.

When all is said, an exposition is a great enterprise whose financial success depends upon the measure in which it pleases, not the artistic few, but the multitude whom it invites through the turnstile. The public wants much and is not critical, and where the practiced architect or the experienced landscape gardener might be inclined to censure, it only approves.

The directors of the Pan-American sought to please the multitude. They took a rectangle of three hundred and fifty acres, and spent ten million dollars in settings—of which, by the way, three million dollars was for a Midway. They have graced their site with a multiplicity of beautiful forms, they brightened it with touches of color, and threw over it the glamour of electrical display; and in view of the fact that the whole is, in the main, highly effective, one can well afford to subordinate criticism of distinctive features to praise.

Many of the sculptural embellishments of the exposition have been given wide currency by the advertising enterprise of the manage-

DON QUIXOTE
By C. E. Dallin

ment. A general survey of the field, however, may here be given. These sculptural features have three great divisions. They open with the magnificent design of the Triumphal Bridge. Then they broaden into the Esplanade, graced on either side by pretentious fountains. Thence they extend through the Court of Fountains to the Electric Tower. The sculpture constituting this elaborate display, though frequently foreign to its environment, subserves admirably the purpose of decoration. The spectator can but admire, though he may not read clearly the symbolic story of the progress which the makers of the groups wished to commemorate.

The Triumphal Bridge is the natural portal of the architectural scheme of the exposition, and is flanked by statues representative of eight cardinal virtues of the nation. These are Truth, Courage, Hos-

MOQUI RUNNER
By H. A. MacNeil

pitality, Justice, Liberty, Patriotism, Tolerance, and Benevolence, and were executed respectively by W. K. Bush-Brown, J. S. Hartley, George E. Bissell, C. F. Harmon, J. Gellert, Gustave Gerlach, H. N. Matzen, and Albert Jaegers. In addition, there are four groups backed with trophies which were executed by Augustus Lukeman.

Both statues and groups are finely conceived and well executed, but one fancies they lose something of their effectivenss from the fact that they are colored in imitation of bronze, a dull hue that looks heavy, and from the further fact that they impress one as being out of proportion with the contiguous towers that are surmounted by Karl

MOUNTED STANDARD-BEARER
By Karl Bitter

SAVAGE AGE
By John J. Boyle

DESPOTISM
By H. A. MacNeil

GAY MUSIC, AND CHILDREN
By Isidore Konti

DESPOTISM
By H. A. MacNeil

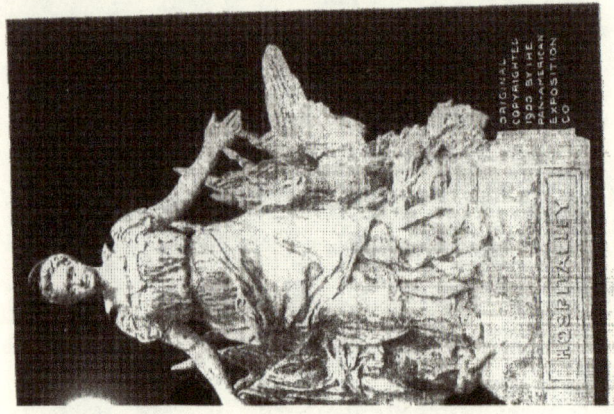

HOSPITALITY.

FIGURE FOR MANUFACTURES BUILDING.

Bitter's four equestrian statues. Of Bitter's magnificent work unstinted praise can be given. His horses are remarkable expressions of spirit and energy. The statues are beautifully decorative in their suggestive movement, and instinct with the spirit of the enterprise for which they were produced. One can but give them the proud distinction of being among the masterpieces of sculpture on the grounds.

The fountain schemes of the Esplanade are especially worthy of comment. Symbolism runs riot in these compositions, as elsewhere, and the spectator feels the need of an interpreter. But the groups are impressive, though one feels the lack of climax in the co-ordination of the principal and the subsidiary pieces.

The chief of these Esplanade fountains are Charles Grafly's Fountain of Man, and George T. Brewster's Fountain of Nature. Both are pretentious and carefully studied compositions. Mr. Grafly's work, near the Ethnological and United States Government buildings, has man for its motive, and is a serious and eminently worthy effort. The sculptor has not allowed the gravity of

THE DIGGER
By Charles J. Mulligan

his purpose to militate against the effectiveness of his composition as a decorative feature. Man's twofold nature is typified by the two surmounting figures whose forms and drapery merge gracefully into a single mass. The senses under the sculptor's plastic touch become youths and maidens, nude and beautiful, who link hands around the pedestal. The conflict of vice and virtue also finds symbolic expression in other groups of male and female figures.

AMOR ON SNAIL
By Janet Scudder

Subsidiary to this central work by Grafly are other compositions, some of which have especial merit. Isidore Konti's Age of Despotism is without doubt the most notable of these. The composition is elaborate, but simple in its suggestion, and is in marked contrast with some of Konti's other groups on the Temple of Music; as, for instance, his Gay Music, in which the spirit is lithesome and festive. In this work the exemplar of brutalism is a man seated in a chariot drawn by other men, whom a female companion lashes with a whip. The symbolism here is self-suggestive, and is sternly, one may say terribly, forceful.

J. J. Boyle's Savage Age and H. A. MacNeil's Despotism of the East are likewise strong conceptions, full of action and passion, and finely executed; while Herbert Adams's The Heart of Man and The Mind of Man are tame in comparison, the ideas exemplified lacking the specific appeal of the more tragic groups.

Brewster's Fountain of Nature, near the Horticulture and Music buildings, is the direct opposite of Grafly's work in its motive. The seasons, the winds, the elements, are Brewster's theme, and hence his figures are more purely symbolic. The four seasons, male and female figures, support a globe, which is surmounted by four other figures, seated,

STATUE OF DR. WILLIAM PEPPER
By Karl Bitter, Sculptor

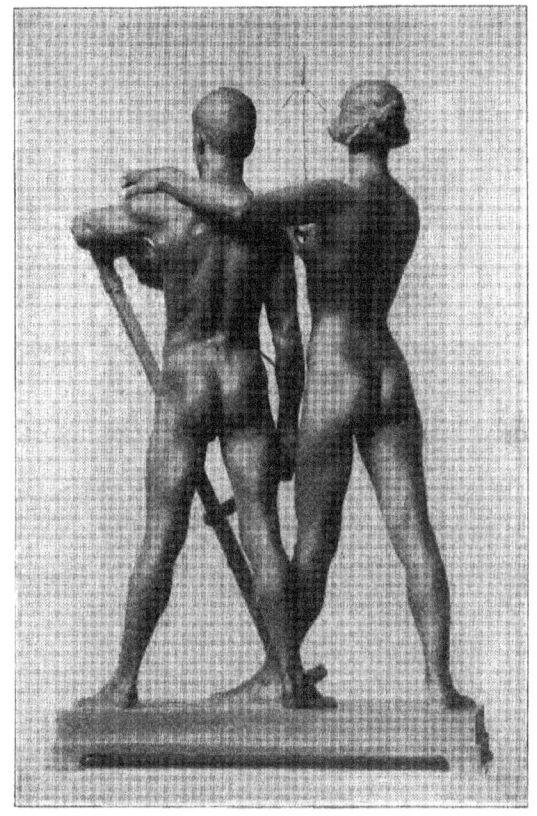

SYMBOL OF LIFE
By Charles Grafly

typifying the elements. The winds are represented at the base, while from the crown of the composition rises the slender, graceful figure of a nude woman. The group is well balanced, and has a charm that inheres in beauty of form rather than of ideas.

As attendants of Brewster's work are Charles H. Niehaus's The Story of Light and The Story of Gold; F. Edwin Elwell's Fountain of Ceres and Fountain of Cronos; Bela L. Pratt's two groups typify-

THE HORSE TAMER
By Frederick MacMonnies

ing Floral Wealth; and E. C. Potter's two groups representing Animal Wealth. The least satisfactory of these secondary compositions are doubtless Elwell's two fountains. The work of Niehaus, Pratt, and Potter is symbolical, pure and simple, while that of Elwell is mythological, a bit of old-world legend in a false new-world environment.

Philip Martiny's Fountain of Abundance, which one greets on turning toward the Court of Fountains, is another bright, festive composition, as pleasing as dolphins and chubby children and a graceful maiden, all treated skillfully and apparently with sportive intent, could make it.

And so one might go through the whole list of the purely decorative statuary with which the grounds and buildings of the Exposition are adorned, and find much to praise unqualifiedly, something to censure, and a great deal simply to take a passing pleasure in. Symbolism—history or fancy in plastic guise—is the keynote of the whole. The beautiful, pure and simple, without a recondite meaning, is conspicuous by its absence.

Phimister Proctor offers a staff representation of Agriculture; Paul W. Bartlett typifies Human Intellect and Human Emotions; Charles L. Lopez gives one his idea in staff of Arts and Sciences; George Grey Barnard publishes two chapters in history in the same material in Primeval Niagara and Niagara of To-day; and so on throughout the catalogue of contributors to the exposition's embellishments and what they contributed.

I found myself trying to discover in some nook or corner a maiden who had nothing to do during her staff life but to look pretty, or some other female in plaster who only sought to look dignified or benevolent; or some male simulacrum who wished only to seem like an interesting human being. But they were all clad in symbolism, though otherwise for the most part nude, and I abandoned the project.

MICHAEL ANGELO
By Paul W. Bartlett

After all, it does not matter much what a figure typifies providing it is graceful, pleasing, ennobling. An artist friend recently submitted for reproduction the picture of a nude young woman standing by the edge of a pond. He wanted the picture called "Autumn." I protested that no sane young woman would do that sort of thing in autumn—the very idea of it suggested goose-flesh or pneumonia. The artist thought so too finally, and decided to call the picture "Spring." It was a pretty canvas, graceful in composition, delicate

LAKE SUPERIOR
By Carl E. Tefft

in color, calculated to charm by its suggestion, and it did not matter what symbolic tag was tied to it—Spring or Summer, June, July, or August, anything but December or March. *Sic* many of the decorative groups at the exposition.

Within the galleries many of the best known American sculptors are fairly represented. Herbert Adams, George Grey Barnard, Paul W. Bartlett, Daniel C. French, Charles Grafly, Frederick MacMonnies, H. A. MacNeil, Phimister Proctor, Augustus Saint-Gaudens, Janet Scudder, Bessie Potter Vonnoh, and other workers in clay and marble—sixty-one in all—contribute liberally. As in the case of the pictorial-art display, however, there is comparatively little in this exhibit of serious work that is new to the public. Most of the groups and statues in the galleries have been exhibited on former occasions, a number of them are medal pieces, and many of them have been presented to the public in former issues of BRUSH AND PENCIL.

Barnard, for instance, sends his two Paris Exposition gold-medal winners; Bartlett, among other pieces, his dignified statues of Michael Angelo and Lafayette; Thomas Shields Clarke, his To Alma Mater; Dallin his Medicine-Man and Don Quixote; French, two of his Hunt Memorial Studies; Grafly, several of his studies that have been exhibited repeatedly; MacMonnies, his Shakespeare that won a grand prize at Paris last year; MacNeil, his two Indian pieces that brought him silver medals at Paris; Proctor, four gold-medal winners at Paris; and Saint-Gaudens, his Paris exposition grand-prize winners.

Space forbids more than a mere casual reference to the galleries' exhibits, which are upward of two hundred in

AN IDYL OF THE PRAIRIE
By Frederick G. Roth

STATUE OF LAFAYETTE
By Paul Wayland Bartlett

number. It may be said, and should be said, however, that the display is thoroughly representative of the work of the best American masters. The directors of the exposition have done well in seeking the loan of so much worthy material, since the serious work naturally supplements the decorative and adds to the educational value of the fine arts exhibition. WILLIAM H. HOLMES.

HORSE TRAINER
By Frederick G. Roth

LONG BEECH-FERN
By Henry Troth
Copyright, 1897, by Henry Troth

ARTISTIC PHOTOGRAPHY OF HENRY TROTH

Even to this day there is no small dissension as to the datum of art. Mr. Whistler's eloquent enunciation of the ultra-impressionistic doctrine continues to be the fetish of one school and the rank heresy of another. On the one hand are the nature-worshipers rallied under the banner of the Slade professor of fine arts; and on the other, the quasi-apologist for nature with Whistler as their leader and his "Ten o'Clock" lecture as their scripture and revelation.

The gulf between the two factions or cults is indeed great enough. Ruskin proclaimed nature as the acme of artistry. But Whistler found that nature merely contained "the elements of all pictures," and was "very rarely right"—"usually wrong"—and "seldom successful in producing a picture." To Whistler, the artist was and is all in all, for the artist's function it is to scan nature's treasury of suggestions, and "to pick, choose, and group with science" the elements therein contained, so that a "beautiful picture may result."

Nature, the base bullion; the artist a refiner; the resulting picture pure gold!

According to either school of thought about art, it is necessary to accord a very high rank to the camerist who is a true artist. Of all artists surely he is most hedged about with difficulties. If he elect to copy nature literally, he must perforce load his result with much that is superfluous; and if he endeavor to "pick, choose, and group with science" a few of the many things in the angle of his *partic pris*, he is embarrassed by the greedy facility of his lens, which cannot eliminate the superfluous or subordinate the lesser object.

BULBOUS BUTTERCUP
By Henry Troth
Copyright, 1901, by Henry Troth

For the lens is an eye in which the philistinism of the Philistine is exaggerated—it sees too much, and is rated excellent in the measure of its capacity for detail, which is contrary to the standards of the artist.

When it happens, therefore, that a camerist *does* succeed in overcoming the deadly redundancy of his instrument—when he develops *in excelsis* the faculty of "picking, choosing, and grouping," despite the handicap of his lens—he deserves all the praise and commendation that have latterly been bestowed on Henry Troth of Philadelphia.

As we might expect of such an artist of the camera, Mr. Troth is able to reconcile in a signal way the divergencies of the Ruskin and Whistler cults of art. He draws the lily, for example, so literally that the result is a competent study for the botanist; but at the same

PHOTOGRAPHY OF HENRY TROTH   283

time he expresses in his work that divine combination of grace and
strength which Whistler was pleased to term "elegant."

Mr. Troth gives us Nature *ipsissima verba* when he deems the

MEADOW SWEET
By Henry Troth
Copyright, 1897, by Henry Troth

language of literal fact to be most fitting; but he reserves always the
option to interpret Nature according to his own innate feeling. He
thus combines the veritistic and the impressionistic in his work, and
is universally acceptable.

In looking through a collection of Mr. Troth's superb photographs,

WILD CARROT
By Henry Troth
Copyright, 1897, by Henry Troth

it readily occurs to any one that he has realized fine possibilities in scores of motives which would have escaped the notice of almost everybody else. We can fancy we see him among a thousand camera enthusiasts roving up and down the New England seacoast, and he alone of all that company pausing to record now and then this slope of sand, that majestic headland, this storm-riven tree-trunk. There is about his photographs a perfect aroma of individuality. Not one of them fails to proclaim his truly artistic selectivity. He discovers peculiar beauties under the obscuring veil of the commonplace, and he has the cunning to make the beauty dominate.

It is a mystery of his craftsmanship how he achieves such successes with material so unprepossessing. In the analysis of his qualities we may say that he has a consummate sense of pure line, of abstract mass, of tonal relations, and of all their combinations and permutations. But he has somewhat more than a mere instinct for the fundamentals of graphic art. He has pre-eminently the rare power of convey-

MOUNTAIN LAUREL
By Henry Troth
Copyright, 1900, by Henry Troth

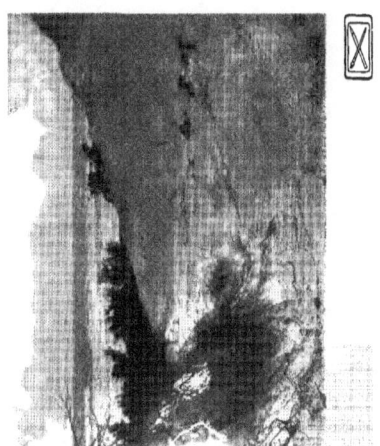

JACK IN PULPIT
By Henry Troth
Copyright, 1901, by Henry Troth

ing suggestions of his poetic moods.

By varying an exposure a fraction of a second and prolonging development a minute or two, he somehow weaves a web of fancy over his negative, and makes the cold platinotype glow with the emotion which sprung up in his heart when he chose his subject. His prize-winning "Sheepfold" picture, recently reproduced in BRUSH AND PENCIL, is a noteworthy example of this faculty. He exhibits it in any number of landscapes and seascapes made on the bleak Massachusetts coast.

Moreover, he has a somewhat Japanese sense of the decorative disposition of simple masses and spaces.

CHICORY
By Henry Troth
Copyright, 1901, by Henry Troth

INDIAN PIPES
By Henry Troth
Copyright, 1896, by Henry Troth

Many of his photographs have *in petto* the quality of mural painting—largeness, breadth, and masterly simplicity. It occurs to some of his admirers that this is his prime forte. No one can study his landscapes without feeling this mural quality. They are fine in ensemble and sufficient in detail.

Mr. Troth's floral delineations are almost uniformly happy in combining the literal and the ideal in just proportion. It is difficult to deal in microscopical minutiæ without falling into the habit of mincing. In handling flower subjects he enlists his decorative faculty, and makes it the foil of his botanical penchant. The fortunate result is, that his pictures are as accurate as leaves from an herbarium, and as pleasing as a cherry-blossom spray by Hokusai—science and art in one.

Finally, he has the manipulative part of his art developed to a degree of perfection which admits of no superior. This is not least of the considerations which prompted his unanimous selection for the jury of the Chicago Photographic Salon of 1901. His presence on the jury of selection vouchsafes the maintenance of high standards, both artistic and technical.

Louis Albert Lamb.

RATTLESNAKE PLANTAIN
By Henry Troth
Copyright, 1897, by Henry Troth

ORIENTAL RUG
From "Rugs Oriental and Occidental"
Copyright, 1901, by A. C. McClurg & Co.

Brush and Pencil

FREDERICK W. FREER, PAINTER

"Beauty is its own excuse for being," says Oliver Wendell Holmes in one of his charming essays, and elsewhere the same genial sage remarks, "All men love all women."

There is nothing novel about these maxims—they are but pat, present-day expressions for ideas that antedate art and love-making. They were, perhaps, as clearly recognized by the primitive artist who outlined his sweetheart's shadow with charcoal, and made the first profile portrait, as by the twentieth-century painters who are now making exhibition canvases of girls in pink or ladies in black or studies of female forms with no clothes at all.

FREDERICK W. FREER
From a Photograph

But there is a direct connection between the two, and the recognition of this connection and the shrewd policy of taking advantage of it for pictorial purposes lie behind many a career in art as the secret of its success. There is a positive delight in that which is simply beautiful—a flower, a sunset, a human face or figure—and be it sentiment or a combination of sentiment and sex, the charm of the female face and form has ever been paramount among lovers of the beautiful. The artist, be he poet, painter, sculptor, who has most deftly used the charms of female beauty in his compositions has made one of the strongest appeals to popular favor.

Tennyson's "Idylls of the King" has more readers than Dante's "Divine Comedy," and the reason is not far to seek—"Beauty is its own excuse for being," and "All men love all women." And so in painting and sculpture, female beauty has been the garment of the ideal—and quite as often the measure of popular success. Many a model has been the making of an artist. Falero, the idealist of stars; Bisson, the painter of a single face; Church, the embodier of moral virtues in plastic beauty; Gibson and Wenzell, the limners of society belles, and other artists legion in number, have learned the value of female beauty in artistic creations and made unsparing use of it. That they have chosen wisely few will doubt, for they have enshrined or given currency to a form of the beautiful that most men hold supreme.

Among the portrayers of female beauty few artists have acquired

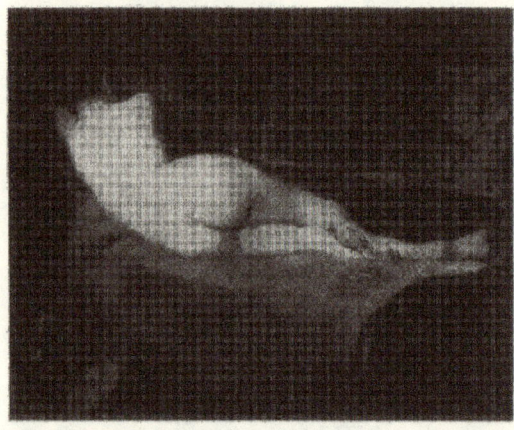

REPOSE OF THE MODEL
By Frederick W. Freer

a greater reputation than Frederick W. Freer. His first great success in oil-painting was the idealized portrait of his model, who afterward became his wife. It was first exhibited at the National Academy of Design in 1887, was afterward purchased by the Boston Art Club as one of its permanent collection, and later won him a medal at the World's Columbian Exposition in Chicago in 1893. This picture, "Lady in Black," now exhibited at the Pan-American exposition in Buffalo, by courtesy of the Boston Art Club, seems to have given definite direction to Freer's energies. It resulted in the production of a long series of paintings whose special charm is the natural or idealized beauty of female faces.

Singularly enough, the reputation he acquired in this class of subjects soon overshadowed that attained in other lines of artistic work. Despite the fact that he is an admirable water-colorist, etcher, pastelist, and portraitist, Freer is commonly known in art circles as the painter of beautiful women's faces. Nobody to-day ever thinks of his water-colors, and yet for years that was the special medium in which he worked and by which he acquired no stinted measure of fame. His etchings, too, are forgotten. A damaged plate hanging in his studio is about the only souvenir

STUDIES
By Frederick W. Freer

of the days when he used the needle. His portraits, painted on commission, are more in evidence—he is now engaged in painting two portraits of Mr. Charles W. Fullerton, one of which will hang in Fullerton Hall at the Art Institute of Chicago.

His favorite art work, however, is that which has given him his distinctive reputation. He is a painter of one model. He painted her on canvas till he painted her in his heart, and he has been painting her ever since, in every imaginable pose and as the embodiment of

STUDIES
By Frederick W. Freer

every sort of idea. The accompanying illustrations will give some idea of the result.

Freer's career is thus a very good illustration of the truth of George Eliot's saying that a straw often gives bent to a life. He was born in Chicago in 1849, and at the age of eighteen found himself a student at the Royal Academy in Munich, where he studied under Wagner, Diez, and other competent teachers. For nearly fourteen years he lived abroad, studying and painting incessantly in Munich and Paris, in Holland and Italy, undertaking various kinds of work and executing everything he undertook with a gratifying measure of success, but never finding the specialty that was to give him distinction.

MEDITATION
By Frederick W. Freer

He returned to New York in 1880, and for upward of six years continued his work, basing his claim to public recognition and patronage largely on his cleverness as a water-colorist. Then chance brought to his studio Miss Margaret Cecilia Keenan. The "Lady in Black" was painted, and Freer stepped to the front as one of the most promising oil-painters of the country. That the chance meeting of model and painter is responsible for the artist's after success, it would be idle to assert. A certain aptitude for portraying the female face, a certain chivalric devotion to his subject, a certain poetic temperament to serve as an interpreter of womanly traits, are necessary for the artist who essays to depict actual or ideal female beauty. Freer had these qualities, and only needed George Eliot's straw to cause him to discover them.

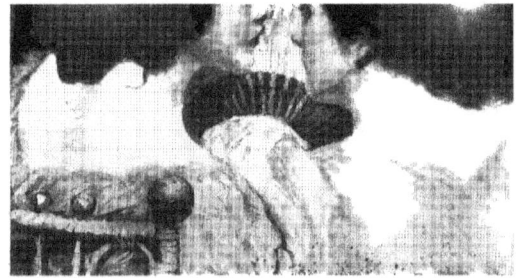

A WHISPER
By Frederick W. Freer

ROMANCE, PASTEL
By Frederick W. Freer

IDEAL HEAD, PLASTER CAST
By Frederick W. Freer

All this, however, is anticipating. A word should here be said of Freer's student days. No student in Munich was a harder worker, and none was a more ardent disciple of the leading spirits of the Munich school. It was from his German teachers that he acquired accuracy as a draughtsman, and it was from them he received a yoke, the peculiar characteristics of the Munich school, which took him years to throw off. It was a wise step for him to abandon the Bavarian art center to sojourn in Paris, where the influence of French art soon became manifest in softness of palette and a pleasing looseness of composition.

It was doubtless an equally wise decision on his part not to identify himself with any of the recognized Parisian schools, but simply to work as a sort of free-lance, studying every phase of art displayed in the French capital and seeking to evolve for himself a style of his own. The direct result of this is that Freer in his mature years—he is now fifty-two years old, but rather glories in the fact that he is still classed with the young men—shows no leaning toward any special school.

His style, his palette, his methods are his own. The sturdy grounding of his Munich days, his deftness and sureness as a draughtsman, formed an admirable basis from which to develop his art by incorporating in it more and more, by strictly individual effort, his own delicate sense of color and his own interpretative perceptions. It has been said of his work that his pictures are grateful alike to the professional and to the unprofessional eye because they have the rare quality of seeming to have been easily done. That this quality is a matter of seeming rather than an evidence of ease of achievement, no one is more ready to admit than Freer himself. He has worked for all he has attained, and his facile brush-work and apparently spontaneous composition are to be taken as witnesses of his devotion to his art and his painstaking industry in obliterating every evidence of crudity and removing all trace of studied change or correction.

"I can say little about my art," said Freer recently. "My interests have changed and my methods have changed with my interests. Just how and why I broke away from the Munich school I do not know, but it seems that I did effectually. For a long time after I followed my own individual bent, they used to call me an impressionist. Some of my work even now savors of impressionism, as indeed I think the work must of any man who undertakes to put on canvas his own views of life and nature.

"Etching with me was something of a fad, although short-lived. Water-color painting was a delight, and on my return from Europe in 1880 I used to work for hours at a time, tacking the paper to the floor and bending over and working out the picture practically between my feet. I was younger then and not so stout, and I fancied that I could get a better command of my colors in that way. Later, when

LAST DAYS ON THE BEACH
By Frederick W. Freer

STUDY FOR CONSOLATION
By Frederick W. Freer

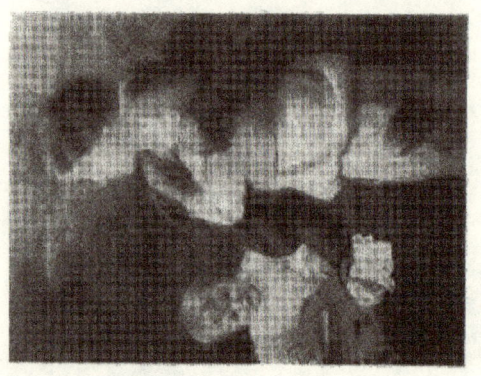

CONSOLATION
By Frederick W. Freer

oil painting engrossed my attention, I worked with a small palette and short brushes. Now I prefer to tack my palette to the easel and work with a brush four or five feet long so as to be almost as far from the canvas as from the model.

"But these are minor details. The essential thing in all my work is, that I arrange my composition carefully, and then with the simplest sort of palette, just a few primary colors, I work out my ideas until the finished result satisfies me. One often hears of authors allowing their tales to grow under the pen. Well, I often follow the same practice. I have started, for instance, to paint a washerwoman at the tubs, and the finished picture has turned out to be a mother fondling her child. So there you are. If you can find anything in my methods that might serve as a hint or guidance to another artist, you can do more than I can."

STUDY FOR PORTRAIT
By Frederick W. Freer

Reverting again to the canvases that have given Freer his distinctive reputation as a painter of women, it is interesting to note that his model for the "Lady in Black" has figured in all his more important canvases. In this original picture he painted a portrait, seeking to delineate on canvas every feature and trait of his model. In every succeeding picture of what may be termed his fair-women series he has renounced strict portraiture and assumed the painter's license to modify or idealize as he chose. It is his wife that he painted in "Consolation," "Young Mother," "Thoughts of the Future," "In Ambush," "Pleasant Musings," and in fact every other canvas in which he has undertaken to exploit the charms of womanly beauty or the traits of womanly character.

It is noteworthy, moreover, in this connection that the artist's facility in modifying, idealizing or otherwise adapting his model's face to his art purpose breaks the monotony of reiteration. One can tell a Henner as far as one can see it, or a Burne-Jones, or a Rossetti, or many another artist who has been slavishly bound to a given model or a given style. No one ever accused Freer of being the painter of "a beautiful woman." His finished pictures are all Freer's, bearing unmistakable evidence of his art, but he has disguised the source of his inspiration.

No one would suspect from a close inspection of his output for the last fifteen years or more that he has juggled with a single face and form and made a single model sub serve the purpose of his artistic creations. That he has done this and done it successfully is no small tribute to his ability as an artist. The idea, the sentiment, the character he wished to depict was in Freer's own mind a matter of strong conception. His model served but as a framework to clothe with an ennobling thought or a pleasing fancy, and in this sense his work is unique. Ridgeway Knight, for instance, has painted innumerable pictures in which his peasant-girl model appears with her simple dress and wooden shoes, but she is the picture and the accessories are Knight's—the flower-dashed foregrounds, for instance, the copses, the glimpses of the Seine, and the broad vistas of meadow beyond. Freer's model is subordinated to a purpose, and her face, to whatever extent it may be true in general details, is masked to suit an idea.

PORTRAIT OF EDWARD KEMYS
By Frederick W. Freer

As an illustration of Freer's versatility, reference may be made to the accompanying illustration of an ideal head in plaster—the only work of the kind the artist ever undertook. This beautiful creation resulted from a mere incident. Freer was appointed to serve on a jury with Miss Julia M. Bracken, who jocosely remarked that it was scarcely right to have a jury with but one sculptor on it. "There will be two sculptors on this jury, Miss Bracken," said Freer, and he left the girl to divine the meaning of his words. He immediately went to his studio, secured the necessary material, and set about making the cast for the ideal head here reproduced. Before the jury sat, the cast, something approximating life size, was finished and exhibited, and Freer posed for the first and last time as a master of plastic art, maintaining his reputation in a new medium as an exponent of female beauty.

THE YOUNG MOTHER
By Frederick W. Freer

As an illustrator Freer is comparatively little known, although he has done much clever work in this special line. In pen-and-ink drawings he evinces the same predilections as in oil paintings. This is a branch of art that he took up after he had scored his first success in the "Lady in Black" as a painter of beautiful women, and his illustrations show an unmistakable effort to carry his taking specialty into the realm of black and white. Many of his illustrations, as, for instance, those for Tom Hood's "Fair Ines" and George Eliot's "Daniel Deronda," are admirable studies of character, having withal in generous measure the same luxury of beauty to be noted in his paintings.

To sum up, Freer is a good deal of a poet in color, with a decided penchant for exp'oiting the beauties of the sex. He is ever refined, ever thoughtful and discriminating. He has never been lured by the nude, except as a studio practice or diversion. His pictures, chaste, delicate, winsome, are thus studies of the sex in the best sense of the term. There is nothing sensuous or suggestive, nothing risque or objectionable about them. Their modernity is pronounced. In some of his illustrations, it is true, he has been guilty of perpetrating cupids with conventional wings and scanty attire, but in his more serious and enduring work, his Hebes, Venuses, and Junos are the Hebes, Venuses, and Junos of the here and now. His ideals are nineteenth or twentieth century ideals. He thinks—and no one will gainsay his judgment—that the artist of to-day has but to look around him for his types of beauty and character, and if, perchance, what he finds lacks the stamp of the ideal, it is the artist's business to think into and paint the ideal into the actual.

Freer is unassuming and retiring, but companionable and popular. Shortly after his return to America in 1880 he was elected an associate of the National Academy of Design, later becoming a member of the American Water Color Society, the New York Etchers' Club, the Society of Western Artists, and other similar organizations. He commands the respect and confidence of his artist associates, and his services are in demand on juries of exhibitions. Nor has he lacked the honors that come from recognized ability. He was the only artist west of New York to win a medal at the Columbian Exposition. He is represented by his work in the Boston Art Club, the Detroit Art Club, the National Academy of Design, the Art Institute of Chicago, the University of Michigan, the Northwestern University, and other public institutions. For some years he has been one of the ablest teachers at the Art Institute of Chicago, being instructor in drawing and painting life and still-life.

FREDERICK W. MORTON.

IN THE STUDIO
By Frederick W. Freer

TYPICAL LANDSCAPE OF THE ORIENT
By H. O. Tanner

POETRY AND PATHOS OF ORIENTAL RUGS

"The time is coming, has already begun to arrive," wrote S. G. W. Benjamin, painter, student, and author, recently, "when Orientals will import steam-made carpets from Europe for their own use; the manufacture of Oriental rugs will then cease as the home demand falls off. Wages in the East will also gradually rise with the general rise of wages the world over, and this in turn will put a prohibitory value on rugs which depend for their chief beauty on manual labor and individuality of expression. And then the Persian rug will become a thing of the past."

Mr. Benjamin would seem to sound the knell of one of the choicest forms of Eastern art. Oriental rugs have grown in popularity for years throughout the Occidental world, and their use in a sense has become a vogue. Their fineness of texture, their durability, their uniqueness of design, the richness and harmony of their coloring, even their pronounced irregularities of shape, which are a witness of the crude methods and plodding toil of their makers, have been prized. While few purchasers, perhaps, would contend that the rugs of the Orient are superior in pattern and finish to the products of Western looms, the use of Oriental rugs in house-furnishing is commonly regarded as an evidence of good taste.

Indeed, to meet the demand for this class of art product, Western merchants have invaded the East, and sought to direct, if not to monopolize, the business of manufacture. They have undertaken wisely, doubtless, to dictate as regards patterns and qualities; but business policy, the commercial sense that attaches value to handmade goods, has restrained them from interfering with the old method of manufacture, and throughout the rug-making districts of the Orient to-day the work is done practically as it was thousands of years ago.

It is to the commercial interest of the West to maintain the old régime. The Orientals are conservative to a fault, slow to grasp new ideas and adopt new methods, enamored, one might say, of crudity and makeshift. And it remains to be seen how long it will take the spirit of the West to pervade the hamlets of the East, cause the rugmakers to revolt against the drudgery to which they have become inured by custom, and realize Mr. Benjamin's prediction.

There is a certain poetry and pathos about Oriental rugs that few purchasers, perhaps, in the West ever think of. The family or tribal legends worked out in the patterns, the religious or ethical meaning to the makers of the blended colors, the toil and privation of which every rug is a witness—these for the most part have been matters of interest only to the student. Little has been printed on the subject of Oriental rug-making. Western lovers of the beautiful only see and admire—and purchase if they can.

A few facts first on the prosaic side of the business of rug-making. Had Hood lived in the East, he would have written the "Song of the Rug," and his "Stitch, stitch, stitch, in poverty, hunger, and dirt," would have been "Tie, tie, tie," etc., with some depressing Eastern monosyllable at the end of a line to take the place of "shirt" and rhyme with "rug." It is woman's work, or was so until recent years, when commercialism impelled a few of the men to take a hand in the business. When we look upon and admire these precious treasures of the East, no two of them alike, each true in general to the family pattern, but all exhibiting the minor license of the individual makers, admiration of the art is apt to blind us to the condition of the women behind it. A few figures may serve to show that art is as long and as poorly paid in the Orient as in the Occident.

A square foot of the best Persian rug is commonly estimated as worth about ten dollars, and an expert weaver working with the regularity and assiduity born of necessity requires twenty-three days for the completion of this portion. The weaver is thus allowed only about forty-four cents a day for her wool and her labor. Three-fourths of this amount goes to pay for the wool, which leaves eleven cents a day for the labor of the artist.

Better wages are earned in producing cheaper goods. An expert weaver can make a square foot of inferior rug, which is sold for about sixty cents, in two days. In this case inferior wool and cheaper dye are used. Though this allows the weaver only thirty cents a day for her wool and her labor, the portion of the amount that can legitimately be termed wages is relatively larger. The poorer rugs, moreover, are twenty or thirty times as large as the superior, which enables the operator to make better time.

On the other hand, the woman who makes cheap rugs works at a disadvantage, since she has to buy her wool, dye it, finish her rug, watch the market for buyers, and bide her time for a sale. The better class rugs, on the contrary, are usually made on order and are paid for when ordered, or at least an advance of pay is made to permit the operator to subsist.

With the reward of from ten to fifteen cents for an average day's work, it can readily be seen that the lot of the rug-weavers is anything but an enviable one. Penury necessitates the simplest fare. An average meal consists of bread, with a little cheese or a raw onion by way of delicacy. In some districts it is even impossible for the weavers to work in the open air, since the excessive temperature dries out the threads and robs them of their elasticity. Hence the weavers are forced into underground places, where they maintain sufficient moisture to keep the wool in workable condition by keeping at hand utensils full of water.

In the West factories are subject to public surveillance, and "sweatshop" has become a word of odium. Many an Oriental rug that we prize as a work of art is pieced out thread by thread under conditions for which a Western sweat-shop could furnish no parallel.

A word as to the different knots used will also be of interest as showing the enormous amount of work involved in the making of a rug. Of course the finer the quality of the goods produced, the closer are the knots. The different "stitches" are as follows: seven by eight, or fifty-six hand-tied knots to the square inch; eight by eight, or sixty-four knots to the square inch; ten by ten, or one hundred knots to the square inch; twelve by twelve, or one hundred and forty-four knots to the square inch; and sixteen by sixteen, or two hundred and fifty-six knots to the square inch.

The woman, therefore, who carries a pattern in her head, and deftly manipulates her threads so as to produce the required harmony of colors for a rug of the best quality, is obliged to tie about thirty-seven thousand knots in making a square foot of carpet, for which she receives as her remuneration the princely sum of two dollars and fifty cents. In short, drudgery, unqualified, unmitigated, by operatives poorly paid, poorly housed, and poorly fed, is the price of every rug over which Western connoisseurs grow enthusiastic. Art affords no more striking example of pathetic conditions. But the women weavers of the East do their work uncomplainingly, since custom has made them content, and contentment is happiness.

Week after week, month after month, year after year, the women weavers of the East sit before their primitive looms—two poles set upright in the ground, with a cross-piece at the top, to which the warp is fastened, and a similar cross-piece at the bottom, on which the finished rug is rolled as it is manufactured thread by thread. Every piece of wool is worked in with the fingers, not with a shuttle, as in the West. There is no guide as to pattern but memory, and hence

HAMADAN CAMEL'S-HAIR RUG
From "Rugs Oriental and Occidental"
Copyright, 1901, by A. C. McClurg & Co.

arises one of the peculiar charms of the Oriental rugs. No two are alike, however much they may resemble each other in a general way. It would not be possible in the whole Orient to find two rugs absolutely identical in pattern.

ORIENTAL RUG
From "Rugs Oriental and Occidental"
Copyright, 1901, by A. C. McClurg & Co.

The work of the weavers becomes almost mechanical. Adaptability to it in a large sense becomes a matter of heredity. The fingers instinctively work in the wool in proper measure and tie the knots

OLD GHIORDES RUG
From "Rugs Oriental and Occidental"
Copyright, 1901, by A. C. McClurg & Co.

with the proper degree of firmness, and the eye detects instantly any lack of harmony in the color scheme that would impair the beauty and richness of the finished product.

The dyeing of the wool in itself becomes an art which one generation transmits to another. It is interesting in this connection to note the peculiar significance attached in different countries of the East to particular colors. The Egyptians regarded black as the symbol of error; white, as the emblem of purity; red, of zeal; yellow, of sorrow; blue, of truth. The Babylonians worked their religion into their rugs, making scarlet stand for fire, blue for air, and purple for water. The Persians have an abhorrence of light shades, and are partial to dark greens and yellows. With them black and indigo represent sorrow; rose, divine wisdom; and green, the initiation into the wisdom of the Most High. The Turks regard green as sacred, and bar that color from their rugs. With the Chinese, yellow is the symbol of royalty; red, of virtue; white, of mourning; and black, of depravity.

And so with the other rug-weavers of the Orient. Their colors are to them a language; and while the expression may seem forced it is nevertheless in a sense true that the weavers work into their rugs a sort of poetry, which only the initiated can read. The same practice is followed to-day as in antiquity, despite the fact that the Western merchants, by the all-powerful means of according or withholding patronage, have made their influence felt in the matter of patterns and colors, just as traders in the Western states have forced the weavers of the Navajo blankets to corrupt the simple, chaste patterns of early days into showier fabrics "that sell."

It would be impracticable in a short article to enumerate and describe the many different kinds of Oriental rugs imported from the East and offered for sale in the Western market. There are dozens of them, each with its own peculiar characteristics in point of pattern and coloring, each also giving evidence of the tribe or family that made it and the source of the wool that entered into its manufacture. The expert trader has but to see a finished fabric to determine from what country or people it came.

One general feature is observable, however, in all work of this class. In modern times and Western nations, finished works of art, as in painting and sculpture, are produced. These works are designed to stand by themselves, without subserving any ulterior decorative effect in connection with other objects. There is, moreover, a craze for novelty, and he who can create a new design or produce a new effect has his reward in a quickly earned popularity.

In the artistic nations of Asia, however, in antiquity all art was decorative, and was meant to serve a utilitarian purpose. The conservative character of the people and their attachment to the past have given persistence to their ideas, and their artistic work to-day is decorative and utilitarian. Indeed, we can find in the rugs of southern Persia to-day practically the same patterns and the same colors as when Ctesiphon was sacked by the Arabs fifteen hundred years ago.

Western manufacturers ransack the world for new ideas, and every

INDIAN PRAYER RUG
From "Rugs Oriental and Occidental"
Copyright, 1901, by A. C. McClurg & Co.

season must perforce bring its new styles. But despite the fact that the production of Oriental rugs runs in families, and each family has its peculiarities, it would not be a difficult thing to trace the genesis of a particular product of to-day back from tribe to tribe and from age to age to early Egypt, which many students think the source of the industry.

Indeed, the early tapestries of Europe and the first carpets of Western manufacture might be traced in a similar way. It will be remembered that carpet-making in the West dates from the reign of Henry IV. of France, when Persian carpet-weavers were brought to Beauvais. That gave impetus to a new industry which has dwarfed in the magnitude of its output the product of the East.

That rug-making in the East should have been one of the most highly prized arts, and should have developed into one of the greatest industries in the Asiatic countries—a great industry in the East is something entirely different from what we term a great industry in the Western world, for the total rug product of the Asiatic countries probably does not exceed a million dollars a year—is scarcely a matter of surprise. The habits of the people, their mode of life, their style of architecture, their customs in the matter of home furnishing, all tended to foster the industry. Rugs are the Oriental's carpets, his bed, his wrappings during periods of travel, coverings for his walls and portières for his doorways, decorations for his temples, mats on which to kneel in prayer, trappings for pageants; in fact, almost everything from purposes of utility to those of high art.

Each nation or district followed its own bent, and trained up its own rug-making families into something like national or district guilds. Some time in the forgotten past the stamp of approval was put upon certain products; some patterns produced by clever workwomen met popular favor, and acceptance of the fabrics was taken as a tacit order to perpetuate them; some combinations of colors struck the Eastern fancy with a similar result, and, we may suppose, some other combinations of colors produced by less skillful manipulators proved an offense to the Oriental eye and were placed under ban, till similar combinations of color became an unheard of occurrence in the industry.

Thus, gradually through the centuries, styles of pattern and schemes of color became fixed. No one will ever know of the daring experiments that resulted in failure and rejection, but we do know that, however numerous these unfortunate experiments were, the accepted patterns and color schemes became limited to a few, so that to-day the entire output of Persian rugs comprises only about thirty patterns. Every weaver, as said before, works in her own little individual variations, which are oftener a matter of chance or accident than design; but for a weaver of to-day to produce a rug with pattern or color scheme in sharp departure from the accepted types that have come down through the ages would be deemed little less than a sacrilege.

The value of an Eastern rug depends on the fineness of the wool, the quality of the dye, and the closeness of the knots, which make a full or a scant pile. The pile speaks for itself to every shrewd purchaser as regards its closeness. The pile of old rugs, however, is often trimmed to remove traces of wear or age. Colors, too, are often doctored by clever workmen who have learned cunningly to touch up with watercolors faded or discolored fabrics, so as to give them the semblance of freshness and richness.

SARAKHS RUG
From "Rugs Oriental and Occidental"
Copyright, 1901, by A. C. McClurg & Co.

The reds are especially subject to this sort of treatment, and the purchaser who is about to invest in a costly rug would do well to rub suspected spots with a damp cloth to detect the fraud.

That all or even a majority of the rugs of the Orient are beautiful, few of Western birth, perhaps, would maintain. But this much must be said of the product as a whole: setting aside all considerations of durability and pattern, the rich, harmonious colorings prompted by Oriental taste are superb. The deep, subdued tones were a revelation when they were introduced into the Western world, and they have had a marked influence on Western decoration. It is to be doubted if the product of the looms of Kidderminster, Wilton, Worcester, Rothdale, Halifax, Dewsbury, and Durham, in England, or of our own Philadelphia, would be what they are to-day in point of artistic coloring were it not for the examples set by the plodding, convention-tied women of the East, who have learned the secret of mixing dyes that last for ages and please without palling.

W. G. MARQUIS.

CONVENTION IN ART

When Japanese art had begun to be known generally in Europe and in America the criticism was frequently made that it was exceedingly conventional. As a matter of fact, it was scarcely more conventional than our own art; its conventionalities were only different from those of Occidental art, and as they were less familiar more notice was taken of them. Many of them have now been accepted and incorporated into Western art, and have ceased to be considered as arbitrary characteristics.

LA MELANCOLIE
Original Engraving by Albert Durer
Showing Conventional Drapery

From childhood we have been taught to make our judgment of artistic representations of every kind, dependent upon a tacit agreement to accept as truthful representation many things which are but little more than symbols, to say nothing of certain broad generalities of such agreements, as that a sculptured figure shall not be expected to

SECTION OF AN ACTRESS
Showing Natural Eye

reproduce color, and that painting may represent three dimensions with two.

One of the earliest known examples of pictorial art was the contour of a mastodon scratched on a bone by a cave-dweller, and in this crude effort of a primitive artist there was conventionality. This instance also shows how artistic conventionalities grew out of the limitations of the artist's materials. One can imagine how the work of this artist of the post-glacial period was received by his friends, the critics of his time. They doubtless saw that the color, size, and hairy covering of the beast were not even suggested, but were willing to excuse this because the artist had done his best with the materials at his command. His rude scratchings were a record of what they had seen in nature, and they recognized that, although imperfect, the picture possessed value.

Lines are constantly used in every form of graphic art, and yet lines do not exist in nature. A contour which simply indicates the boundaries of a form is accepted as a representation of it. But forms in nature are not bounded by lines. In drawings and etchings masses of lines become tones and values to those who have been educated to regard them as such, but the untrained eye sees the spaces between

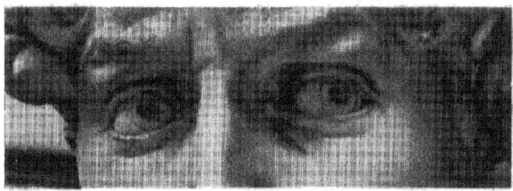

PART OF THE HEAD OF DAVID
By Michael Angelo
Showing Sculptured Eye

WOOD-CUT. By Albert Durer
Showing Conventional Drapery

and often fails to appreciate their meaning. In a painting the same value or tone would be represented by an even wash of color or a mass of pigment, and the observer must replace the standard by which he judged the drawing with another one based on other conventions.

Relation is an important factor in artistic representation. A relative scale of values of dark and light is imposed by the limitations of the materials an artist uses. White paper or white pigment is not so light as a clear sky, and yet painters attempt to represent even the glowing light of the sun or of flames. A stroke of pure ivory black or of the

JAPANESE WATER-COLOR
Showing Use of Shadow
Courtesy of H. Deakin

blackest of crayons produces a gray which is extremely dark by comparison with other pigments, but which is far lighter than the blacks which are found in nature. This is clearly demonstrated by photography.

A relative scale of dimensions in both pictorial and plastic representations is so common, that it would be childish even to speak of it as an artistic convention, were it not for other accepted conventions which have grown out of the fact that the scale is not and cannot readily be consistently adhered to. A few examples will illustrate this.

In a landscape blades of grass are represented by brush-strokes which, according to the scale of other objects in the picture, might be an inch in thickness, and yet we have learned to accept the result as the symbol for grass. The like is true of the leaves of trees, hairs, feathers, and other small objects.

EARLY JAPANESE PRINT
Showing Absence of Shadow
Courtesy of H. Deakin

On the other hand, a flat mass of paint is accepted with equal readiness as a truthful representation of assemblages of the same objects in another painting of similar scale. Many Japanese painters are less conventional in this matter. Instead of suggesting grass by a few strokes which are out of scale or a mass of proper color, they laboriously fill their foregrounds with masses of brush-strokes proportionate to the size of other objects represented.

Curiously enough, there is a tendency to consider present artistic conventions, when once accepted, as final, and to regard any departure from them or any innovation as illegitimate art. It was not so long

HEAD OF CHRIST
By S. Cecilia Cotter
Showing Smooth Hair, Suggestive of Light Color

ago that it was not considered proper to use white or opaque color in a water-color. Here was a case where a range of values could be extended considerably, and consequently be made more closely to approach nature, but both artists and the public had learned to believe that unity of material was of primary importance, and barred change.

CONVENTION IN ART 315

The invention of photography was a death-blow to many conventionalities of drawing. When artists first drew running horses in poses which instantaneous photographs had taught them to see, the public, which had known only the conventional hobby-horse poses, with four legs extended as a symbol for speed, was unwilling to accept them as truthful. But there was at the same period a blind faith in the veracity of all photographs, and they were at length accepted under protest as truthful, but ugly. To-day the photographic poses are the only ones which are recognized as correct.

The Japanese observed the flight of birds, and gave truthful representations of it before the Occidental artists had conceived the idea that there was any other way to represent the flight of a bird than by raised and extended wings, and yet any child could have told them that "what goes up must come down." Photography finally convinced them that the Japanese artists had been less conventional than themselves in this matter.

The limitations in values of light and dark imposed by the range of the palette have so long been considered fixed that any attempt to extend them is considered tricky and false. As it has been already suggested, absolute white and absolute black have not yet been produced in pigments, and yet if a landscape painter, after having "played the limit" in attempting to reproduce the actual values of nature, should resort to the use of tinsel, as scene-painters sometimes do, to produce a high light, he would call down censure upon his work if his methods were discovered. By the ethics of painting he is constrained to paint only such subjects as call for a limited range of actual values, or fall back upon the conventionality of a relative scale.

The realists who preceded the impressionist school attempted to reproduce the

BIRDS FLYING.
Showing Actual Poses, from Photograph.

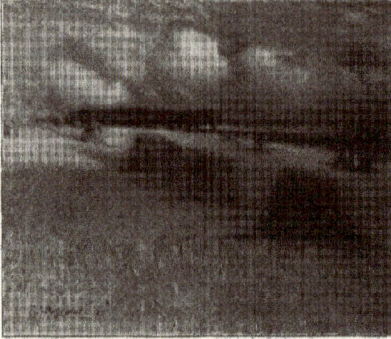

LAST GLOW
By F. C. Peyraud
Bright Sky in Art

actual values of nature. Their efforts in this direction resulted in the abandoning for a time of sunlight effects, which they deemed unpaintable. Then came the impressionists who painted shadow as nearly true as possible to its actual value and sunlight as light as possible. An effect of luminosity was gained, but the truth of the scale of values was lost, and thus a new convention was established.

To-day there is a clearly defined tendency toward tone pictures of

GRAY DAY AT CUSHING'S ISLAND
By Charles Francis Browne
Dull Sky in Art

a range of actual values easily within the scope of the palette. With a system of relative values few pictures are painted in the same scale. The same actual value of paint may mean something entirely different in one picture from what it does in another. For example, in a gray-day effect and in a sunlight effect the artist will use the highest possible value to represent the highest lights and the strongest darks obtainable in paint to represent the darkest shadow. And yet in the

SUNSET IN THE ADIRONDACKS
By Earl Deakin
Bright Sky by Photography

effects seen in nature there exists a wide difference between the respective lights and shadows.

The fact that the mixing of colored pigment with white lowers its value, makes it often possible to paint the almost colorless sky of a gray-day landscape actually lighter than the blue sky of a sunlight effect, or even the red orb of a sunset.

If the relation of the middle tones and tints between the notes of the highest light and deepest shadow is preserved, the result, by convention, is called truthful. The realistic effect of a panorama painting is due simply to the fact that all points of comparison are removed, and much that is real in the foreground in front of the canvas is given a false value to make it in harmony with the range of values of the painting. The actual earth piled up there, for instance, is mixed with lamp-black to make it match the painted earth of the foreground of the canvas.

It has been a convention of Japanese art that shadows are a defect of nature, and difficulties were avoided by not representing them, particularly in the works of the painters of the older schools. Most of the modern artists of Japan who have not adopted the methods of European artists in great measure have learned something of the use of shadows from them.

RAIN FROM THE SEA
By A. Horsley
Gray Sky by Photography

The conventionalities of sculpture are even more apparent than those of painting. A basrelief is perhaps the most striking of plastic conventionalities—a sort of compromise between a picture and a statue. The third dimension is often suggested only a little more than in a painting. Some painters give a relief to objects in the foreground of their pictures by imposts which might be considered another combination of the two arts. The attempts to suggest color in sculpture have given rise to several conventionalities. One frequently sees a statue in which only a representation of form is given in every detail except the eyes, in which the pupil is represented by a round hole, and the high light which glistens in the living eye is suggested by a bit of marble or bronze left at the top of the hole. Blond or dark hair is suggested by smoothness, which reflects light, or by broken masses presenting many small shadows. These effects of partial representation of color are so familiar in statuary that they are not considered inconsistent.

A few of the conventionalities of art, some of which we have outgrown, have been mentioned. An inspection of the art of earlier periods will reveal many others. The treatment of drapery in various periods shows a long sequence of conventionalities, and furnishes an interesting study in itself. Decorative art is made of conventionalities, but it is the purpose of this article to call attention only to those which exist in the branches of art which are commonly supposed to be free from them. Why should attention be called to them? For the reason that a knowledge of their existence may promote a better understanding between artists and laymen. The truth which artists are striving for is a higher truth than an exact representation of nature. Art

THE FALCONER
By Eugene Fromentin
Showing Conventional Horse Pose

should furnish food for the imagination. It should be a poetic expression. The works of realistic painters are chiefly interesting from the fact that it is impossible for them to be absolutely realistic. There is always a personal note.

Again, if we know of the conventionalities which already exist in art, we may be more lenient to the artist who may develop new ones. An artist who goes out to nature, and develops something new from

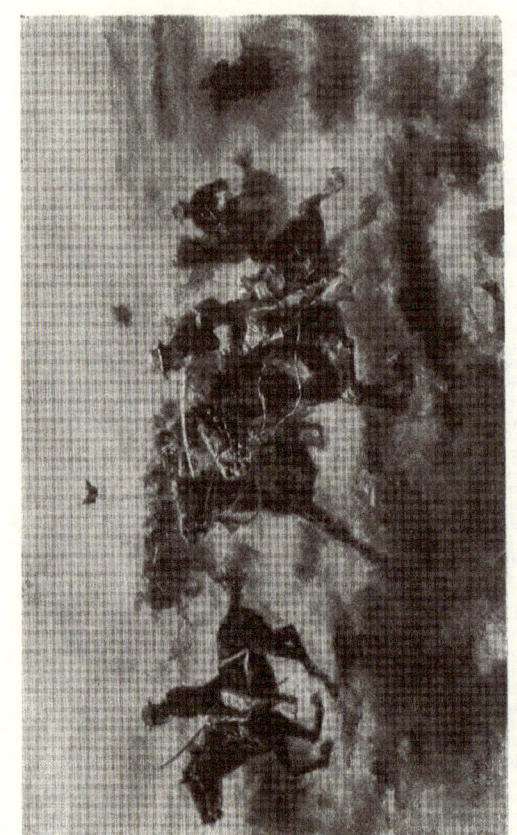

AT CHICAMAUGA PARK
By F. C. Yohn
Copyright, 1898, by P. F. Collier
Modern Heroic Pose in Art

NATURAL HORSE POSE
From a Snap-Shot Photograph

the inspiration he receives there, is generally condemned as a falsifier. He may have ignored old, familiar conventions or invented new ones. In a few years he may be hailed as a master. Millet, Corot, Delacroix, Manet, Bastien-Lepage, Whistler, Rodin, and Puvis de Chevannes are a few who have been both reviled and glorified.

EDGAR CAMERON.

BRIDGE OF DON, ABERDEENSHIRE, SCOTLAND

BRIDGES, ARTISTIC AND INARTISTIC

No artificial feature of European landscape is more pleasing to the tourist than the æsthetic character of its bridges, and no feature of the American landscape is a greater abomination. Throughout Europe, with occasional exceptions, these monumental public works, spanning rivulet, river, and gorge, seem to fit into and form an essential part of the scenery. In America the same class of structures is for the most part a disfigurement.

In the one case, we are rarely conscious of a discordant element in the picture presented. In the other, we feel that man has perpetrated a blunder, and deliberately marred the beauty of nature. European bridges, in a word, impress one as having been constructed, consciously or unconsciously, with direct reference to art; American bridges, on the other hand, seem to be mere contrivances for the convenience of travel, in which the idea of utility is so dominant as to preclude the very thought of grace and fitness.

Nothing can be more charming in the British Isles and in the continental countries than the innumerable stone arched structures we find thrown across streams and ravines, mellowed by time and decorated with lichens, their lines often the very embodiment of grace, and their solid masonry apparently as enduring as the hills among which they nestle. Even bridges of comparatively recent construction in the great European cities seem to have been patterned after these earlier "rule of thumb" bridges, as modern engineers have been pleased to term them, and an effort seems to have been made to combine utility with the principles of æsthetics.

BRIDGE OF THE PO, AT TURIN

As a rule, the older the bridges, the more they antedate the engineering era, the more beautiful they are. The old structures are the work of architects who studied the conformity of the land and who sought to plan something fitting and harmonious. Modern engineers, with these early examples of structure before them, have endeavored to bend their steel trusses into lines of beauty and clothe them in such a way as to disguise the baldness of mechanical device. That they have been fairly successful, none are more willing to admit than American engineers and bridge-builders.

In this country we have had no antiquity during which bridge-builders worked by the "rule of thumb." In the pioneer days utility was the sole idea to be compassed. The straight truss, the most inartistic of all bridge conceptions, was thrown across short spans. Economy and time were regarded as paramount issues by the prosaic bridge-builder, and art scarcely commanded a thought.

NORMAN BRIDGE OVER THE MOOSE, LANARK, SCOTLAND

Later in America, bridge construction became little more than a matter of engineering feat. Bridge-builders scoffed at the achievements of early architects, who used many arches to span a comparatively short space, and gloried in their new-found ability to cover an enor-

CARTLANE CRAGS BRIDGE, LANARKSHIRE, SCOTLAND

mous space with a single span. It was once deemed a notable event to throw an arch over a three-hundred-foot gorge or stream; it is now a comparatively easy trick to span a space three thousand feet wide.

The slow mastery of the art of bridge-making in the Old World, and its gradual evolution under new conditions and new methods of structure, are thus apparent throughout Europe in the later and more pretentious bridges. The poverty and crudity of pioneer days in America, the necessity of studying cost and economizing time, and the quick development of engineering enterprise in later days are observable throughout this country.

American bridges are not things of beauty—they never have been; and if the ambitious spirit of engineering enterprise continues, which delights to tempt the impossible, throw precedent to the winds, and accomplish feats by means more novel than pleasing, it is to be doubted if, with rare exceptions, they ever will be. The critics of the Old World, therefore, who come to this country have no hesitation in saying—and saying with sincerity—that American public works, and especially American bridges, are executed without any reference to art whatever. They wonder at our enterprise, our ability, our ingenuity, and at the same time deplore our lack of taste.

This is scarcely to be wondered at. Our achievements in the matter of bridge-building are the work of engineers who have rejected the associate services of architects, and who have been even more disdainful of the suggestions of artists and art lovers. "Of those public works," said a competent writer recently, "which, by necessity or custom, are confided to engineers rather than to architects, bridges are the most conspicuous, and it is in bridges that the reference to art is felt most gratefully by its presence in Europe and most painfully by its absence in America."

This is the age of iron and steel, and in a sense the age of stone is dead. It may seem, therefore, the cavil of querulousness to find fault with a form of structure that has been forced upon the world by a combination of conditions that did not exist when many of the artistic bridges of the Old World were constructed. But the contention is rightly maintained, that if the modern bridge-builders of Europe can preserve in their steel, present-day structures something of the grace and charm that obtained in ante-engineerng days, there is no reason why we in America should scorn to profit by early examples, and should build so many unsightly structures devoid of æsthetic qualities.

It may be, occasionally, that the exigencies of demand may require some remarkable performance of engineering ability under conditions that do not lend themselves to æsthetic treatment. But these are the exceptional cases. For every one bridge built in America under conditions that make the "rule of thumb," or ancient method of procedure, impracticable, hundreds are built under conditions that make it entirely possible to observe the closest reference to art. There is no reason why so many of our bridges should be eyesores—blots on the landscape. Indeed, the sins of inartistic con-

KINZUA VIADUCT, AMERICAN BRIDGE

OLD SUSPENSION BRIDGE OVER NIAGARA RIVER

struction are most observable in the minor bridges, for which conditions were favorable for fine treatment, than in the greater structures.

It is to be noted that in the greater bridge enterprises of America there is a grace, a charm of form, wholly lacking in the less pretentious affairs. To span the East River, for instance, in New York, offered almost insuperable difficulties; yet the Brooklyn bridge has a beauty of outline apart from that suggested by the wonder of the achievement. The same is true of the great bridge spanning the Mississippi at St. Louis, in which the lines are as beautiful as those of many

BRIDGE OF THE INVALIDES, PARIS

of the European bridges that are famous the world over.

And yet over many a narrow span, where a due regard for the natural features of the land and an adequate consideration of architectural form might result in a structure of surpassing beauty, a real enhancement of the landscape, we find an abomination of a truss bridge, or some other form of unsightly iron structure that is unsuited to the landscape, and that depends for its existence on repeated painting and patching.

WELLESLEY BRIDGE, LIMERICK, IRELAND

SECOND BRIDGE, VIA MALA (GRISONS)

The greatest offenders in the matter of bridge-building in America have doubtless been the railroads, and a competent English critic has attributed to our enormous and progressive railroad enterprises much of the evil as regards bridges of which complaint is made. The charge seems to be fairly well founded. In the Old World railroads came as the culmination of former unsatisfactory means of travel. Macadam highways and graceful arched bridges of enduring masonry antedated them by ages; and while in many instances the railroads renounced old models and resorted to novel and inartistic means

BRIDGE AT CLUSE, ON THE ARVE, SAVOY

of spanning stream and chasm, precedents of the bridge beautiful were in existence in numbers, and acted as a salutary influence to prevent the multiplication of unsightly structures.

In America, on the contrary, the railroad, after the prairie schooner, was the invader of the wilderness. The main object in mind was to provide a means of transit; cheapness and rapidity of construction were factors of importance; the country was unsettled, and hence looks did not count; there was no thought of the future of the territory invaded, and consequently no consideration was had of fitness or beauty of structure. Straight trusses, double bow-string or lenticular trusses, steel arches, cantilevers, pivotal swing bridges—anything was used that lent itself most readily to the mere purpose of utility. The aims of the railroad enterprises were subserved, and the ends of art were ignored.

The unsightly railroad structures having been erected throughout the country, they formed prototypes for the lesser bridges needed on highways and byways, and these multiplied with the development of the districts traversed, until there is little room for marvel that European visitors, accustomed to the beautiful public works of their own countries, should denominate us a people shorn of artistic conceptions.

I have no desire to institute invidious comparisons, but it is almost impossible to refrain from comparisons in considering the subject. Suppose, for instance, a straight truss or an inartistic cantilever bridge were substituted for the second bridge, Via Mala, or for the Devil's Bridge, Canton Uri, Switzerland: the means of transit would be subserved just as adequately as by the artistic stone arches, pictured herewith, that span the chasms; but art would be damned forever. Or suppose spindling truss bridges were to replace the bridge at Spoleto, Italy, or the Cartlane Crags Bridge, Scotland, both of which by their massive arched structure suggest alike the thought of beauty and of durability: the landscapes would be robbed of features as picturesque as the hills and valleys themselves. Or suppose that under the caves of Notre Dame, in Paris, as shown in our illustration, there were in place of the graceful sweeps of the arched bridges a couple of monstrosities like the State Street bridge in Chicago, herewith presented: we should gain, perhaps, a suggestion of traffic, force, energy, but the beauty of the Parisian scene would be lost forever.

Of course we cannot shut our eyes to the fact that circumstances, the necessities of enforced requirements, alter cases, and that a style of construction eminently fitted for one place or one purpose would be wholly inexpedient for another. But it may be urged with equal force that in this day of steel structures, as in the days of the "rule of thumb" bridges, the manner of construction may safely be left to the engineers, but the form of the finished structure cannot be so left. There is need of the work of competent architects, and in Europe at the present day architects do take a hand in all such public works, and undertake to plan appropriate structures to fit specific needs.

This is one of the main points on which American bridge-builders are weak: they presume to dispense with the architects, and let utility

BRIDGE BETWEEN DULUTH AND WEST SUPERIOR

or the mere exigency of mechanical construction so dominate the work as to kill every suggestion of art. That this is a needless sin against taste scarcely needs demonstration.

The cantilever bridge as we see it in America, for instance, is for the most part a structure as devoid of beauty as is the simple straight truss bridge. That this results from a needless disregard of artistic principles has been amply shown by European bridge-builders. Compare the beautiful Mirabeau cantilever bridge, in Paris, the sweep of whose arches is as graceful as that of any "rule of thumb" bridge of antiquity, with the great cantilever bridge over the Niagara River in this country. This latter structure, as shown in the accompanying cut, cannot by any license of courtesy be called beautiful. An engineering feat it certainly is, but it impresses one as a homely, spindling, utilitarian span, and nothing more. There is not a line of beauty about it. As excuse for this, the builders will doubtless refer to the breadth of the chasm and the difficulty of spanning such a distance. This, however, would be but begging the question. The real trouble is a deliberate renunciation of æsthetic principles.

Had the builders of the bridge over the Niagara River had the same reference to art as did the builders of the Mirabeau bridge over the Seine, there is no reason why the former structure should not rival the latter in its artistic features. The cantilever bridge over the Hudson River at Poughkeepsie is equally hopeless from an artistic standpoint. Primarily, the cantilever bridge is but a straight road-bed supported by brackets, and the successful treatment of the brackets, the shaping of them on lines of beauty, as in the Mirabeau bridge, in Paris, is all that is necessary to make this form of structure as artistic in its effect as the stone arches of antiquity.

HENRY T. WOODBRIDGE.

TO BE CONCLUDED.

VICTORIA BRIDGE

CANADIAN ART

The Pan-American Exposition has brought conspicuously to public attention a phase of American art that has been developing slowly and surely, but without so much as a passing notice of its existence. I mean the work of Canadian artists.

The art exhibition of the provinces in the Albright galleries is not extensive—only forty-nine artists are represented by eighty pictures—but the collection is eclectic in the best sense of the term, and it is thoroughly representative of the best efforts of the Canadian painters. Fully half the contributors are connected with the Royal Canadian Academy, whose members, through their officers, Robert Harris, G. A. Reid, M. Matthews, and James Smith, have taken a commendable pride in showing the high class of work now being done in their country.

We, in the United States, with our larger and broader art interests, are apt to overlook, and perhaps even disparage, the art products of the Canadian provinces. Many readers, doubtless, do not even know that there is such an institution as the Royal Canadian Academy, and those who know of its existence perhaps fail to realize that in the measure of its opportunities this institution is striving zealously to stimulate and broaden the art spirit in Canada and to promote every form of art interest.

That this work of the Academy is attended by difficulties and discouragements is frankly admitted by the officers of the institution. It is chiefly in the provinces of Ontario and Quebec that one can speak of an art spirit at all. Many of the best artists of these provinces have of recent years left the country, lured by what they thought were the brighter prospects offered by the populous cities of the United States. The market for high-class work in oil and watercolors in Canada is narrowly circumscribed, and as a consequence there has been a tendency for years toward the depletion of Canadian studios. The artists move away and soon are utterly lost to their country, since change of residence has in most cases involved the assumption of new allegiance, the artist claiming little more than Canadian birth.

The same is true of those who have made illustration a specialty. The publishing interests of the provinces are meager and can give but scant employment to promising men. In consequence there are probably fewer competent artists in Canada to-day than there were a decade ago.

Canadian artists have the same complaint as their American confreres, that the collectors and connoisseurs of their own country, who spend thousands of dollars annually in works of art, are prone to slight native talent and devote their money to the purchase of Old World products by recognized masters. This, however, is less surprising than in the case of artists of the United States. As was recently pointed out by one of the closest observers of Canadian art interests—and a Canadian himself—it is only of recent years that the art of Canada has passed beyond the production of fairly well exe-

CANADIAN ART EXHIBIT
Pan-American Exposition

cuted water-colors depicting still-life subjects or topographically correct bits of landscape.

It is not to be overlooked—and the fact should be noted in justice to the public—that those Canadian collectors who have expended large sums for foreign art works have felt a sense of obligation to foster home talent and have been the most liberal patrons of the colonies. In a word, Canada has been in the position of most colonies the world over. It has received slight and patronizing recognition from Englishmen in general, and virtually no recognition from the residents of other countries. Under these circumstances, it is somewhat surprising that native artists have made such satisfactory progress. In

DESDEMONA'S PALACE ON GRAND CANAL, VENICE
By Frank Duveneck
Courtesy of Albert Roullier

GALLERY OF ETCHINGS
Plate Seventeen

reviewing the development of Canadian art during the last decade, M. L. Fairbairn said recently:

"Our national art institution, the Royal Canadian Academy, during these ten years has pursued the even tenor of its way, filling the vacancies made by death or removal, holding its yearly festival, staid, respectable, slowly progressive, adding to the permanent collection in Ottawa the diploma pictures of its new members. The number of exhibits each year has not increased, because in former times each academician was entitled to have twenty pictures hung, no matter what their merits, so the walls were always covered. The number has since been reduced to ten, and later to eight. The standard for the works of outsiders has been raised, so that with fewer pictures the exhibitions are better."

The same characteristics that Mr. Fairbairn speaks of as obtaining in the last Canadian exhibition are observable in the exhibit at the Pan-American. Canadian painters have been brought under the influence of all the art influences of recent times. This is partly due to the fact that many of them have received instructions from masters in leading schools outside their own country and partly to the practice of importing and exhibiting in the leading cities of the provinces examples of the best work of American and European artists. Canadian artists have thus fallen into line in all new movements, following instead of leading, it is true, but nevertheless giving evidence of an alertness to what is going on in the art world to-day and a desire and a capacity to profit by the examples which they have not yet been able to set.

This is conspicuously shown in the work of the various art schools throughout the provinces. These schools are increasing in number and efficiency, and they find an able auxiliary in the Women's Art Association, which has developed with remarkable rapidity during recent years, and which now has branches in a number of the leading cities throughout the provinces of Ontario and Quebec.

Interest in the art work of the better known schools is also markedly advanced by the development of an arts and crafts movement in Canada. Lovers of the beautiful were not slow to take inspiration from William Morris, who sought to apply art to the requirements of daily life. The direct result of Morris's influence has been to impel Canadian artists to supply designs for the manufacturers of their own country and to inaugurate various exhibitions of applied art and design. A higher standard of taste has thus been developed as regards both fine and applied art, and this higher standard of public taste, for which the artists themselves are responsible, has reacted upon themselves and of necessity impelled them to higher attainments.

The Canadian art exhibition at the Pan-American shows the fruits of this healthful condition of affairs. Of the eighty pictures displayed, many are of an exceptionally high quality, showing broad, truthful treatment and mastery of technique. William Brymner shows three charming water-colors, two of which, "The Gray Girl" and "Francie," are finely executed figure-studies. "The Gray Girl" presents a little miss in the attitude of writing, and "Francie" portrays a sunny-haired child standing in natural posture against a dull gray background. In both pictures the color scheme is low-toned, harmonious, and eminently pleasing. F. M. Bell-Smith also displays three characteristic pictures, "London Bridge," "Strawberry Pickers," and "Above the Clouds." These show a wide range of interests, and a capacity for different types of work that augurs well for the future of the artist.

J. L. Graham's three pictures, "Dinner-time in a Stable," "Ploughing," and "Carting Sand," show a marked ability to invest homely scenes with poetic character. His "Carting Sand," depicting two horses pulling a load over a heavy road, with a couple of countrymen walking beside the wagon, is an especially worthy interpretation of country life. Robert Harris, president of the Royal Canadian Academy, who won a medal at the Chicago exhibition, and also an honorable mention at the Paris International Exhibition a year ago, exhibits two fine portraits of women, suggestive of a close study of Gainsborough.

In the line of portraiture, E. Dyonnet, E. Wyly Grier, who took a third medal at the Paris salon, A. D. Patterson, and G. A. Reid also exhibit fine canvases, which betray a delicate palette and a firm grasp on the essentials of good portraiture. "The Beach of St. Malo," by James Wilson Morrice, is especially pleasing in tone and subject, as is also "Girl Knitting," by Laura Muntz, in which sunlight effect is most admirably depicted.

G. A. Reid, also a medalist at the Chicago Columbian Exposition, exhibits a choice decorative panel, "Summer"; F. M. Knowles, two fine pictures of the Thames River and an equally choice canvas, "The Last Load"; William Cruickshank and F. S. Challener, familiar farm scenes; M. A. Bell and John Hammond, marines; and H. Blair Bruce, a dainty canvas depicting nude maidens sporting on a moon-lit beach.

Other canvases are no less worthy of mention, and space alone forbids further specific mention. Suffice it to say that W. E. Atkinson, J. A. Brown, Henri Beau, W. D. Blatchly, F. H. Bridgen, Maurice Cullen, Florence Carlyle, J. W. Forster, J. C. Franchere, R. F. Gagen, C. S. Haggerty, Homer R. Watson, Mrs. Mary Heister Reid, Edmund Morris, C. J. Way, F. A. Verner, William Hope, M. Matthews, and other leading artists of the provinces are represented by pictures ranging from still-life to landscape, and from portraiture to *genre* subjects. These pictures, do not suffer by comparison with the work of other American artists.

KATHERINE V. McHENRY.

www.ingramcontent.com/pod-product-compliance
Lightning Source LLC
Chambersburg PA
CBHW030254240426
43673CB00040B/970